EVERYTHING IS CHESS

Bernie Ascher

authorHOUSE®

AuthorHouse™
1663 Liberty Drive
Bloomington, IN 47403
www.authorhouse.com
Phone: 1 (800) 839-8640

Published by AuthorHouse 05/10/2018

ISBN: 978-1-5462-3258-2 (sc)
ISBN: 978-1-5462-3256-8 (hc)
ISBN: 978-1-5462-3257-5 (e)

Library of Congress Control Number: 2018903126

Table of Contents

Dedication

This book is dedicated to the author's #1 fan:

Sandra "Sandy" Langbein

and

the Ascher and Langbein families

Acknowledgements

The author wishes to thank all the friends, neighbors, and relatives who encouraged him to write these articles and to publish them in book form. Apologies to all those not mentioned here by name.

For their assistance, special thanks go to the editors and staff of Leisure World News, particularly Maureen Freeman, Stacy Smith, Kathleen Brooks, and Cassandra Chisholm, as well as Arthur N. Popper, Chairman of the Leisure World News Advisory Committee. Mark Weinberg drew comical illustrations for an early version of the book.

The book owes its origin to the Leisure World Chess Club, whose members checked out the puzzles first before reading the articles. The late Professor Clay McShane was among the first to recommend a book of articles. Harold "Hal" Kern, Donald Wendell, Gary Weiner, Lark Keller, and Steve Harvith may recognize some of their end games in the puzzles. Pat Leanza prepared the chess diagrams in the early issues.

The group of Romeos gave the author moral support (Arthur Nimetz, Norman Jacobs, Gerald Wolf, David White, Richard Riseberg, and Jacob Rothmel). Stewart Lillard and Palma Seeger provided tips on publishing. Avid readers Robert and Lorraine Levan provided valuable advice and sympathy.

Schoolteacher Sandra Langbein assisted in many ways, with ideas, good grammar, and laughs, bringing the author back down to earth when necessary.

Preface

Leisure World of Maryland is a gated community for active adults over 55 years of age. It is conveniently located in Silver Spring, Montgomery County. The community has two clubhouses (including one with restaurants, a ballroom, a post office, and a credit union), indoor and outdoor swimming pools, a golf course, tennis courts, a fitness center, a transportation center with three bus lines, a medical clinic, and an interfaith chapel.

Many of the residents engage in sports, dancing, and other physical activities. Management is very much concerned with the health, safety, and well-being of residents. Thus, while walking along the paved walking paths, signs remind residents against "roller skating, roller blading and bicycling." One sign reads: "Do not climb on the rocks."

In the gym, residents wear colorful T-shirts with inscriptions, like Tigers, Warriors, and Demons, or colleges, which their grandchildren attend at high cost. They proceed to work out furiously on the exercise machines, after setting aside their canes and walkers.

A hollow, 40-foot, world globe at the main gate marks the property. Security guards operate the main gate, which is open 24 hours. Guardhouses, each of which closes at 10 pm, are at two other locations. The gates are intended to allow bona fide visitors to enter (not to keep the residents inside). Residents are free to leave at any time without a visa or passport. Those returning after 10 pm must enter the main gate. It is not true that residents must explain why they are late. (They do not get a lecture for returning at that hour, but they may get a stern look from the guard as if they had done something naughty.)

The speed limit on the smoothly paved roads within the community is 30 miles per hour, except for seniors in bright red convertibles with the top down. Golf carts always have the right of way, on the sidewalks as well as the streets. Residents celebrate July 4th with parades and speeches by politicians. In the parade, a truck hauls a flat bed with eight seated musicians ("The Leisure World Marching Band").

The community also has its own newspaper, library, education, and recreation center. Leisure World News is devoted to publication of news and information for the benefit of residents of this active adult community of 8500 people. There is a club for almost every interest, including woodworking, health, theater, religious and ethnic affiliations, and hobbies--- such as the Chess Club, which brings us to this publication.

Chess Club members meet three times a week, more often than they see their own relatives. They develop a bond of friendship and are always seeking new members. It is difficult to attract new members because chess competes with golf, bridge, and woodworking. The ordinary "Brief Notes" listed in the newspaper were not very successful. Thus, the Club launched the idea of writing chess articles on a regular basis to call more attention and sign up more players.

Since 2009, the author has been writing a chess column for Leisure World News. The author's best friends, neighbors and relatives prevailed upon him to publish a collection of columns as a book. It took very little to convince the author to comply.

At the start, the articles largely addressed chess--- with catchy headlines to gain attention. "Chess on Mars," for example. The trick was to show, in a humorous way, how chess related to the exploration of Mars or whatever was the subject, and to tie it all together so it made some kind of sense.

Who should read this book?

- All 45 million chess players in the United States
- Anyone else who enjoys a good chuckle or two

The author has a split personality: ordinarily, he is a soft-spoken, humble, retired government economist and international trade professor; occasionally, however, he is an outspoken critic of life's ironies and trivialities and a rabid chess enthusiast.

As you will discover, the author's view of the world today is that there are too many countries, too many languages, too many words, too many regulations, too many taxes, but not enough time to play chess.

When asked why he named this book "Everything Is Chess," the author replied that he thought "Chess Is Everything" would be too presumptuous a title.

Introduction

"Everything Is Chess" is an amusing collection of essays on current events and world history as seen through the eyes of an avid chess player with a sense of humor. It is mostly non-fiction and explores a wide variety of diverse subjects, including the following.

- **Celebrating holidays** --- Christmas deliveries are complicated for Santa; not everyone lives in a detached single family home with a chimney.
- **Naming and numbering wars** --- If armies had better technology, the Hundred Years War could have been completed in 100 days or less.
- **Re-naming the Redskins** --- If we called them the Red Kings, only monarchists would be offended.
- **Collecting taxes** --- It seems almost sacrilegious that the tax code is now 5 times larger than the Bible.
- **Strengthening sanctions on Russia** --- Obama could forbid Putin from dancing with Michelle at international social events and Germany and France could do the same for Angela Merkel and Christine Lagarde.
- **Remembering the Titanic** --- While the band played and the ship went down, chess games continued in the game room.
- **Surviving for a week on a cruise ship stranded at sea** --- Investigators discovered that the ship was not adequately equipped with chess sets for use during such an emergency.

- **Discovering dinosaur bones** --- Even Endangered Species Legislation could not have saved them.
- **Counting world population** --- There are more sheep than people in New Zealand. Whose fault is that?

It asks (and sometimes answers) impertinent questions.

- **Does chess cause wars?** (Although chess is full of strategic planning, traps, trickery, attacks and captures, there is no evidence that it incites violence.)
- **Do Popes play chess?** (Chess is not one of the requirements for the Papacy.)
- **Which U.S. President was the best chess player?** (Except for his assassination and skills at chess, President Garfield is known only for his picture on a 20-cent postage stamp.)
- **How can American presidential election campaigns be simplified?** (Have the candidates play each other in a chess tournament.)
- **Is Columbus Day celebrated in Italy?** (Italy favors Columbus over Rossini, Michelangelo, and Gina Lollobrigida, none of whom has a holiday of his or her own.)
- **How could General Petraeus have avoided a scandalous love affair?** (He should have played chess instead.)

Some questions are more directly linked to chess.

- **Is chess better than baseball?** (You don't need eighteen people and acres of land to play chess.)
- **How should one dress for chess?** (You need not wear a helmet or other protective gear.)
- **How can chess be modernized?** (Instead of Kings and Queens, the pieces can be transformed into corporate executives or professionals--- CEO, COO, CFO, doctors, lawyers, engineers, etc.)
- **Is there a word for checkmate in Esperanto?** (*Mortigas* is the word for checkmate (to immobilize) and chess is *sako* (pronounced shahko)).

- **How is chess treated in the media?** (Chess never made it on radio);
- **Why should we be thankful for chess?** (One of the ten reasons is that it gives us something to teach our grandchildren when they teach us how to use mobile electronic devices.)
- **Is chess kosher?** (Unless it is edible or touches food, chess need not be kosher.)

These articles, originally intended to attract new members to the Chess Club, appeared in Leisure World News of Maryland. Each column included a chess puzzle and solution. The core of each article, however, was commentary on a topical subject. The trick was to tie each subject to chess in a humorous way. This was accomplished with a short segue into the puzzle and a conclusion, urging players not to procrastinate, but to play chess now (for example: do not wait for Congress to act; do not wait for a puff of white smoke from the Vatican; do not wait for Columbus to discover America again! Play chess now!)

As the column progressed, more non-players began to read it. Currently, non-players outnumber players as readers.

Foreword

Benjamin Franklin's Chess Ethics

April 5, 2015

If Benjamin Franklin lived in Leisure World, he would be a member of the Chess Club. Yes, in addition to all his other accomplishments, Ben was an ardent chess player. During his years in Paris, Ben was known to play chess from evening until dawn.

Franklin wrote an essay on the Morals of Chess, which was published in 1786. "The game of chess," he wrote, "is not merely an idle amusement; several valuable qualities of the mind [foresight, circumspection and caution are] useful in the course of human life…" In 1999 (yes 1999), Franklin was inducted into the Chess Hall of Fame in Miami, Florida (posthumously of course).

His essay remains a good example of etiquette of the game. Most Leisure World chess players observe these morals even today--- whether they know it or not.

For example, Franklin emphasized that both parties must play by the rules, and that no false moves should be made [no cheating]. Basically, LW Chess Club members abide by these ethical rules. However, some players may fall short of following several of Ben's other morals, such as "do nothing to hurry or distract your adversary…" Or "you…ought not deceive your adversary by pretending to have made bad moves and saying that you have lost the game in order to make him secure and careless, and inattentive to your schemes, for this is fraud and deceit, not skill in the game of chess." Interesting, isn't it, that such psychological warfare tactics were used in chess as far back as the 1700s?

And there must have been kibitzers back then, too, prompting Franklin to write that "if you are a spectator while others play, observe the most perfect silence, for if you give advice you offend both parties..."

But, most important, players at the Leisure World Chess Club are good sports and show behavior consistent with one of Franklin's ethical rules: "You must not, when you have gained a victory, use any triumphing or insulting expressions, nor show too much of the pleasure you feel, but endeavour to console your adversary, and make him less dissatisfied with himself..." After a tough struggle, all LW players congratulate their opponents for a good game, believe it or not.

If you want to check this out, play a "friendly" game (don't kibitz) at the Chess Club in Clubhouse II between 1 pm and 4 pm on Monday, Wednesday, or Friday. There is no need to bring your own set. The Club has ample supplies. The Chess Club also has a library of chess books, which has recently expanded, thanks to generous donations from its members. For further information, call our Club President [name and phone number deleted]. Membership is free. Be a good sport, like Ben Franklin!

Do Popes Play Chess?

March 18, 2013

Thanks to the media, we know a lot about newly elected Pope Francis I. He is 76 years old, one of five children born in Argentina to parents originally from northern Italy. He is a Jesuit, committed to serving the poor. (Yes, of course, the Pope is Catholic.) He is a model of austerity, modesty, and humility. He has only one lung (resulting from removal of an infected lung during his childhood) and he loves the tango and futbol (soccer).

What we do not know is whether or not he plays chess. (What is becoming of journalism these days?) History tells us that seven of the previous 265 Popes played chess (according to chess.com and other sources). In chronological order, here are the Popes who played chess (and the years of their reigns): Pope Gregory VI (1045-1046); Pope Innocent III (1160-1216); Pope Leo X (1513-1521); Pope Paul III (1534-1549); Pope Leo XIII (1878-1903); Pope John Paul I (Aug-Sept 1978); and Pope John Paul II (1978-2005).

Specifically who played chess with the Popes is not known, but one book reports that an 11th century Pope played chess with Rabbi Rav Shimon, the chief rabbi of Mainz, Germany ("Can I Play Chess on Shabbas?" by Joe Bobker.)

Chess, of course, is not one of the requirements for the Papacy. In fact, religions have not been kind to chess over the centuries. Various religions have banned chess from time to time in several countries. In ancient days, religious groups regarded chess as idolatry due to the carved chess pieces, which resembled "graven images." The clergy considered chess a wasteful activity, which interfered with daily prayers. Also, about 1400 years ago, chess was played with dice and was considered gambling.

Chess became a problem in India in 900. Players wagered fingers in chess matches. The loser actually would have a finger cut off. During the Inquisition in Spain in 1495, live persons would represent chess pieces. As the pieces were captured, those representing the pieces would be put to death.

Chess was banned for a time in Egypt (1005), Russia (1093, 1551), Paris (1125, 1198, 1208), Worcester, England (1240), and Germany (1310). In some instances, the prohibitions were aimed solely at Catholic priests, as for example, in Rome (1215).

For fear that it would lead to gambling, Rabbi Maimonides included chess among the forbidden games for Jews around 1195. By 1500, however, chess became a Sabbath pastime for Jews, as long as it was not played for money or with a time clock.

More recently, in Iran, Ayatollah Ruhollah Khomeini prohibited chess in 1981, presumably because it encouraged gambling. Recognizing the high educational and intellectual values of the game, the Ayatollah changed his mind and issued a religious decree (fatwa) in 1988, permitting chess play for Muslims as long as it is not played for the purpose of gambling and it does not delay the obligatory prayers or neglects other duties. Thereafter, Iran organized a chess federation promoting chess education and tournaments for young people.

The Leisure World Chess Club does not use dice in playing chess and members do not worship the pieces. In the case of some players, however, prayer is the only way they can win.

So, do not wait for official approval. Do not wait for prayers. Do not wait for a puff of white smoke from the Vatican. Play chess now!

Patriotism and Chess

June 18, 2013

As we observe Independence Day on July 4th, it is appropriate to examine the linkage between chess and patriotism. International chess tournaments are generally organized according to national teams. Oddly enough, there appears to be some controversy over this.

Many believe that players thrive on the excitement of belonging to a group and representing their country. A national team gives identity to a group of players and stimulates interest of observers and chess fans. Others believe that chess is a game of high intellectual quality which transcends nationalism and that nationalism denigrates the character of the game.

Over the years, numerous chess champs and other famous players have played for countries other than the country of their birth. Russians played for France (Alekhine, Tartakower, amd Bernstein), Poland (Winawer and Rubenstein), Germany (Bogolyubov), and Denmark (Nimzowitsch). Germans (Mieses) and Austro-Hungarians (Gunsberg) played for England. Czechoslovaks (Flohr) and Hungarians (Lilienthal) played for Russia. Obviously, there has been considerable migration of players from country to country.

There is no controversy about organization and patriotism at the Leisure World Chess Club. Players are not organized along national lines. In fact, there is no organization at all. Chess is played just for the fun of it--- and for the intellectual exercise as well.

No question of patriotism arose in the LW game pictured on this page. White is threatened by Black's Queen and Bishop along the a1h8 diagonal. What is White's best move?

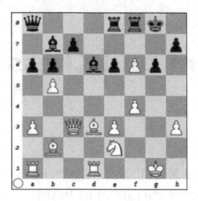

Solution to Puzzle #1 appears on Page 247.

So do not wait for a speech by the four-star General. Do not wait for a flag pin to place in your lapel. Do not wait for the band to play the national anthem or Stars and Stripes Forever. Play chess now!

Wrestling: Yes, Chess: No

October 1, 2013

Wrestling is back--- but then again, it never really left. Seven months after the International Olympic Committee (IOC) removed wrestling from the list of core sports for the 2020 Olympics, the ancient sport was reinstated in the 2020 games, after beating out baseball, squash and a long list of others. Wrestling also beat out karate, roller sports, sport climbing, wakeboarding and wushu (martial arts).

To regain Olympic status, FILA (the governing body for international wrestling) and its new Serbian President promised to speed up the matches, change the scoring, add more women's weight groups, and make other crowd-pleasing adjustments to the rules, such as changing the color of the mats, redesigning the uniforms, and wrestling shirtless. (Note that Olympians originally wrestled in the nude.)

This is naked commercialization. In the future, can we expect to see mud wrestling and wrestlers sporting "Hulk-Hogan-style moustaches"? Will we see more body slams, biting, choke holds, and other dirty tactics? We may have to wait until 2020 to find out.

Meanwhile, chess remains outside the Olympics because the IOC does not recognize it as a sport--- despite the efforts of the International Chess Federation in the 1920s. The IOC regards chess as a game, not as a sport. Shucks!

But chess can still be played in ordinary, comfortable, casual clothes as in Leisure World's clubhouse.

So do not wait for the 2020 Olympics! Do not wait for international recognition! Play chess now!

Christopher Columbus Discovers Chess

October 15, 2013

Columbus Day is not celebrated in Italy. It is celebrated, however, in New York, Baltimore, and other cities in the United States with large Italian populations. Columbus was born in Genoa before Italy became a nation-state. He believed that one could reach India by sailing to the west of Europe. Many people at the time thought Columbus was crazy because it was common knowledge at the time that the world was flat and that westbound ships would fall off the edge before they could reach India. The world was not yet ready for global positioning (GPS).

Columbus was financed by Queen Isabella and sailed under the Spanish flag. This explains why Columbus Day is celebrated in Spain, and not Italy, but it does not explain why it is celebrated by Italian-Americans in the United States.

Columbus was about 41 years old when his ships arrived in Hispaniola---what is now known as the Dominican Republic and Haiti (although Columbus believed he was in Asia). He never really landed on the U.S. mainland, which is probably why he lost the naming rights to Amerigo Vespucci.

In the United States, Columbus Day became a national holiday in 1937. Originally, it was celebrated on October 12, not because it was Columbus' birthday (which is October 31), but because that was the day he landed in the Americas. Beginning in1971, as a result of Congressional action, Columbus Day has been moved to the second Monday of October, regardless of whatever day of the week Columbus actually landed.

Reportedly, Columbus and his crew brought chess, checkers and other games to the New World. To this day, many people play chess every day in many places, including Leisure World.

So, do not wait for Columbus to discover Leisure World. Do not wait for an Act of Congress. Do not wait for a new Vespucci Day holiday. Play chess now!

[Note: On October 12, 2004, Italy began celebrating Columbus Day as a national holiday.]

Modernizing Chess for Television

November 19, 2013

Chess is an old game. It was invented before television. Some say there is a need to modernize the game to make it more entertaining as a spectator sport in the 21st century. Here are some ideas.

Start by modernizing the chessmen and chess women. Kings and queens are old-fashioned. Monarchies are no longer in vogue. They are important only in a historical or cultural sense. So the chess pieces themselves need to be redesigned.

Instead of representing warring parties of different kingdoms, for example, the chess pieces could be designed to represent competition between rival multinational corporations. Instead of kings, queens, knights and castles (rooks), the game could feature key corporate executives--- CEOs, COOs, CFOs, Board and Committee Chairpersons, lawyers, accountants, engineers, security guards, computer specialists, and human resource managers. Similar to checkmating the King, the object of the game would be to put the rival corporation out of business.

Under another approach, taking a cue from present-day computer games, chess could be represented as a battle between extraterrestrials and earthlings. Imagine all the different kinds of creatures that could appear on the chessboard. The outcome of the game would determine whether or not control of the planet will go to the invaders from outer space.

In addition, the chess pieces need not be simply black and white, they can be multi-colored, like flags. The players themselves could wear uniforms to symbolize their affiliations, their nations, or their neighborhoods. In fact, the individual players could be formed into teams. Each move would be preceded by a huddle. Bring on the cheerleaders.

To inject more action into the game, chess needs more bodily contact and more penalties for unsportsmanlike conduct. How to accomplish this in a tasteful way befitting this great game will take exceptional skill and creative thought.

Meanwhile, chess games at Leisure World continue in the old-fashioned way, as illustrated by the diagram on this page. In this game White can check Black's king by moving the Rook to c1. However, it is Black's turn to move. What is Black's best move?

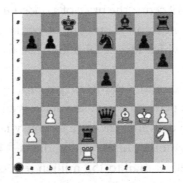

The solution to Puzzle #2 appears on Page 247.

So, do not wait for chess to be modernized. Do not wait for a new cast of characters. Do not wait for chess to become a crowd-pleaser on high definition TV. Play chess now!

How Chess Can Save the Postal Service

January 21, 2014

It is January now and U.S. postal rates are going up again. It is becoming an annual ritual. Later this month, the price of a first-class letter will increase by 3 cents to 49 cents; the price of a once-famous penny-postcard will increase by one cent to 34 cents. The object is to generate $2 billion for the postal service, which lost $15.9 billion last fiscal year.

Except for birthday cards and wedding invitations, people just do not want to write messages with pen and paper, and address envelopes by hand, and buy stamps to pay for delivery. They are too busy keeping up with their cell phones, e-mails and other high tech products. Meanwhile, the postal service is obliged to deliver mail to 152 million residences from businesses and charities that want your money and are willing to pay for delivery (but not enough).

Postal authorities are overlooking a good, potential source of revenue: chess game correspondence. At one time (when postcards cost a penny), lots of people played chess by mail. The government needs to find a way to revive chess correspondence. This could generate billions of dollars in revenue. Consider that 35 million people play chess in the United States and that an average game consists of about 40 moves per person or 80 moves per game. A single game would generate $27.20 in postage at 34 cents per card. Multiply this by 35 million. This would produce $952 million. So, chess correspondence alone could raise about $2 billion, if the government could motivate all chess players to play two games per year by mail.

To provide an incentive for correspondence chess, the government could establish a million-dollar competition. The players who won the most games or sent the most postcards would be awarded a million-dollar prize. The media probably would provide lots of free publicity, as they do for lottery jackpot winnings. Otherwise, the government could use the "health care" approach by requiring all chess players to register and to play two games per year by mail or pay a hefty fine.

At Leisure World, you will not find Chess Club members writing each other postcards. They play chess in "real time."

So, do not wait for the next postcard. Do not wait to hit the jackpot. Do not wait for postal revenues to balance costs. Play chess in "real time" now!

Why Chess Is Not in the Winter Olympics

January 29, 2014

Chess is not a winter sport. It is difficult to play chess while sledding, skating or skiing, but that is not why chess is excluded from the Olympics. Chess is not recognized as a sport by the International Olympic Committee (IOC) because it is considered a game, not a sport. The IOC maintains that there is not enough physical activity for chess to qualify as a sport.

The IOC and the TV broadcasters may be missing out on a unique opportunity. With a little ingenuity, chess can be adapted to winter sports and can add new interest to the Olympics.

Picture this. The scene is an ice skating arena filled with spectators. Two skaters enter the rink. One is dressed entirely in white; the other completely in black. They skate to the center of the rink. A referee, wearing black pants and a white-and-black striped shirt, joins them. They bow. The crowd greets them with applause. The white-clad and black-clad players skate to opposite ends of the arena.

The referee carries a chess board with pieces all set for a game. The music starts. (It is Johann Strauss' Blue Danube Waltz.) The referee skates toward the white player, holding the chess board and pieces on a tray in one hand over his head like a restaurant waiter. His skating is so smooth that it does not upset one chess piece on the board. He sets the board on a tall table before the white skater.

While the white skater is considering his first move, the black skater begins a skating routine. (The music is Edvard Grieg's In the Hall of the Mountain King from the Peer Gynt Suite.) He executes a perfect Lutz jump and a spin and returns to his end of the rink.

White completes his first move. It is posted on the video scoreboard. The crowd is hushed. The referee then skates to the other end of the rink with the chess board and Black considers his response while White skates to center ice and performs a routine to the tune of Gioachino Rossini's William Tell Overture. He finishes with a spectacular triple axel jump. The crowd cheers.

The process continues as each player alternates skating and chess and the referee transports the board between them. The crowd cheers each performance and each move. The winner of the chess match gets interviewed by Bob Costas. ("How pleasing was this victory for you?" "What thoughts went through your mind after your opponent's twentieth move?") If the game ends in a draw, Bob Costas interviews the referee.

Meanwhile, half a world away from the Sochi Olympics, chess continues at Leisure World. Here chess is played year-round without fanfare, without special costumes and music, but with friendly competition.

So, do not wait for snow. Do not wait for the next Winter Olympics. Do not wait for chess to be recognized as an Olympic sport. Play chess now!

Iran, Sanctions, and Chess

February 4, 2014

Iran is a four-letter word, meaning "Land of the Aryans." Every crossword puzzle fan knows that. Iran has a long history in chess. Some say the game may have been invented there. In fact, the English term "checkmate" (the final move of the game) is based on the words "shah mat" in Farsi, "death of the King."

Iran has been subject to economic sanctions by the United States for more than three decades--- since Iran's revolution in 1979, when the Shah was overthrown and hostages were taken at the U.S. embassy in Teheran. These sanctions have been tightened progressively in recent years as a means of limiting Iran's capability of developing a nuclear weapon. The sanctions consist of freezing Iran's assets in the United States and other restrictions on finance, investment, and trade with Iran. Last year, the sanctions brought Iran to the negotiating table to discuss the peaceful use of nuclear power with the United States and other member countries of the United Nations. (It is unclear why Iran, a country with vast reserves of oil, needs nuclear energy anyway.)

The sanctions have affected Iran's second-leading industry (after petroleum): the automobile industry. Those of us, who have never seen an Iranian vehicle, never would have suspected that it actually had such an industry and was a leading auto producer in the Middle East. Due to sanctions, however, Iran's auto industry has fallen on hard times. Production has dropped drastically, perhaps by 40 percent. An official of the Iran Vehicle Manufacturing Association told reporters last October that "many workers in the factories are just sitting around or playing chess," according to an article in the Washington Post.

With this information, we now know how sanctions could be tightened even more to bring pressure on the Iranian government. If somehow we could prevent Iranians from playing chess, the idle workers would have time to organize demonstrations against the government. Think of all the protesters carrying signs in the streets of Teheran. "Bring Back Chess!" "Liberate Chess!" "Chess is Freedom!" Iranians who are hooked on chess will be outraged! Yes, this is the kind of issue that motivates people. Denial of the opportunity to play chess may be the ultimate sanction for Iran.

Meanwhile, here at Leisure World, residents are free to play chess on a regular basis, as in the game pictured on this page. In this game White is one move away from promoting its Pawn at c7 to a Queen. However, it is Black's turn to move. What is Black's best move?

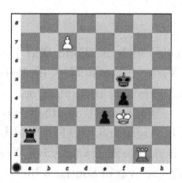

Solution to Puzzle #3 appears on Page 247.

So, do not wait for a political movement. Do not wait for Iranian auto workers to protest. Do not wait until the end of economic sanctions. Play chess now!

Does Chess Cause Wars?

April 1, 2014

History is full of wars. Most of them have unimaginative names. Generally the names are based on the combatants in the war (the Franco-Prussian War, the Russo-Persian War) or the location of the war (the Vietnam War, the Korean War, etc.). Some war names are based on the year of the war (the War of 1812) or the duration of the war (the Thirty Years War, the Eighty Years War).

Some wars are numbered, such as World War I, which was known as the Great War or the War to End All Wars, until the Second World War came along. Also, some wars have more than one name. What is known as the French and Indian War in the United States is known as War of the Conquest in Canada. In Argentina, the Falkland Islands War is known as Guerra de Las Malvinas. The American Civil War is also known as the War Between the States, the War of Southern Independence, and the War of Secession.

One of the more imaginative names is the War of Jenkins Ear. Robert Jenkins was captain of the British merchant ship *Rebecca*, which was boarded in 1731 by Spanish coast guards, who severed his ear. The ear was preserved and presented to the House of Commons during debate in 1738. The British were offended by this act and declared war on Spain in 1739.

(These matters moved more slowly in those days due to lack of proper technology. In fact, if modern transportation and communication had been available at the time, the Hundred Years War might have been

16

completed in one hundred days. Modern technology makes everything more efficient.)

Surely, we can be more imaginative in naming our wars today. Some colorful names might include: "the Mistaken Identity War," "the Missing Uranium War," and "the Electronic Surveillance War." Perhaps what is needed is a United Nations War Naming Commission.

There is great concern about violence in movies and video games because it could incite young people to commit crimes and become the cause of wars. But many wars occurred before the invention of movies and videos. Chess can be considered as a source of violence if one regards strategic planning, traps, trickery, attacks and captures as "violent." Even though chess existed prior to motion pictures and computers, however, there is no evidence that chess actually has caused wars. Combat on the chessboard is more symbolic than real. There are no explosions and no bloodshed.

Chess is played peacefully at Leisure World and opponents generally shake hands at the end of each game. In the game pictured on this page, Black has more pieces and it is Black's turn to move. What is Black's best move?

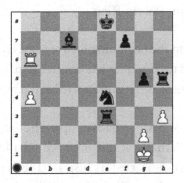

Solution to Puzzle #4 appears on Page 247.

So, do not wait for diplomacy. Do not wait for appeasement. Do not wait for sanctions. Do not wait for a U.N. resolution. Play chess now!

Baseball, Australia and Chess

April 15, 2014

Fans who believe that baseball is America's national pastime may be surprised to learn that this year's major league opening day game was played in Sydney, Australia. On March 22, the Los Angeles Dodgers beat the Arizona Diamondbacks there, 3-1. Attendance was a respectable 38, 266 (even though ticket prices were high). This was the seventh time Major League Baseball opened the season outside continental United States. Previously, games were played in Monterey, Mexico; Tokyo, Japan (4 times); and San Juan, Puerto Rico.

To watch this game from the beginning on live television in the United States, viewers would have had to turn their sets on at 11 p.m. on the west coast (2 am on the east coast) inasmuch as the game started at 8 p.m. in Sydney's time zone.

You probably knew that Sydney had an opera house, but did you know it had a baseball park? Actually, it did *not* have a ball park until this game was scheduled. The city converted its historic 1880s facility, known as the Cricket Grounds, into a baseball field in 16 days, using over 150 tons of concrete to remodel the stands and outfield walls and 200 tons of clay to build the infield and pitcher's mound.

Contrary to popular belief, even though the game was played "down under" in the Southern hemisphere (where water supposedly empties from the bathtub in a clockwise rotation rather than counterclockwise), players did not have to run the bases clockwise, that is, backwards from third to second to first to home instead of the regular way around.

(By the way, in the interest of full disclosure, it should be known that the bathtub "vortex" is now believed to be a misunderstanding of the phenomenon known as "the Coriolis effect." The effect does influence certain large things like air masses over long periods of time, but the immediate effect is so small that it plays no role in determining the direction in which water rotates as it exits a draining sink or toilet. So, the next time you happen to be in Australia, you might check this out. Also, while you are there, check out whether the sun rises in the west and sets in the east and whether there are more sheep than baseball fans there.)

At Leisure World, chess is played year-round, so there is no need for opening day ceremonies. Chess is easier to play than baseball. You do not need acres of land, fences and foul poles. You do not need special equipment, such as baseballs, bats, and gloves and you do not need 18 people to play a game. Only two players were involved in the chess game pictured on this page. In this game, Black has a passed Pawn on e-3, which is threatening to become a Queen. Black also has two strong Knights. It is Black's turn to move. What is Black's best move?

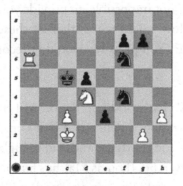

The solution to Puzzle #5 appears on Page 247.

So, do not wait for next year's Opening Day. Do not wait for Australia to join the major leagues. Do not wait for the Washington Nationals to win the World Series. Play chess now!

World Population and Chess

May 20, 2014

It is a generally accepted fact that the world's population has exceeded 7 billion. There is disagreement, however, on when this occurred. The United Nations Population Fund contends that the milestone was reached on October 31, 2011. The U.S. Bureau of the Census believes it occurred on March 12, 2012. We may have to learn to live with this uncertainty.

Nobody is asking for a recount. After all, it is difficult to count such a large number of people. Counting the first billion might take thirty years, especially if the population is marching before you in single file.

It is equally difficult, if not impossible, to provide you with a picture of the world's population. How would you gather all these people in one place to pose for the camera? (You probably wouldn't recognize anybody in the photo anyway.)

By 2050, it is expected that world population will reach 9-10 billion. The World Health Organization is concerned that continuing growth of the population will create food shortages and lead to higher prices. This revives the issue that made Reverend Thomas Malthus famous for his failed theory that world population would outstrip the food supply by the mid-1800s.

Malthus, of course, did not foresee all the scientific and technological advancements developed since then, including the discovery of broccoli. Malthus deserves credit, on the other hand, for looking ahead and sensing a future problem at a time when the population was much smaller than it is today.

The significance of world population growth for chess is that there will be more chess players to contend with in the future. Chess at Leisure World will not be endangered by world population growth and will continue as always.

In the game accompanying this article, Black's major pieces are huddled in one corner. It is Black's turn to move. What is Black's best move?

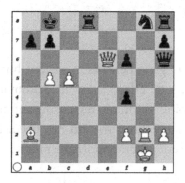

The solution for Puzzle #6 appears on Page 247.

So, do not wait for the next Census. Do not wait for world population to decline. Do not wait for lower food prices. Play chess now!

Telephone Solicitations
and Chess

October 7, 2014

Technology has brought great benefits to society, but upon occasion there have been undesirable side effects as well. Automatic telephone dialing systems are a case in point. Telemarketers, using automatic dialing systems, are trying to sell you something you do not need. Moreover, unwanted telephone calls usually come at inopportune moments. They interrupt you and annoy you.

Congress has come to the rescue with enactment of the Telephone Consumer Protection Act of 1991, which is the basis for a Do-Not-Call Registry (administered by the Federal Trade Commission with the cooperation of the Federal Communications Commission). You can try to protect yourself by getting your name and phone number on the list, but this does not always work.

However, a different approach might bring some measure of revenge and might even prove to be more effective. When you answer the phone and say "Hello" and there is no immediate response, it is usually a telemarketer who has dialed multiple numbers and is slightly late getting to your line.

Here is what to say when you hear the voice at the opposite end. (Speak in a halting monotone voice, like a robot.)

"You have reached the number that you dialed. If you are a human, press 1. If you prefer Spanish, press 2. If this is an emergency, please hang up and dial 911.

"This call is being recorded for quality purposes.

"Please listen carefully to the following menu as the choices change frequently. If you are calling to tell me I won a prize, press 1. If you are calling to sell me an extended warranty on my old car, press 2. If you are calling to lend me money, press 3. If you want me to send you money, press 4. If you are calling to straighten out my credit, press 5. If you want to clean my carpets, press 6. If you want me to buy electricity cheaper than PEPCO, press 7. If you are calling from India to fix my computer, press 8. If you want me to vote for your candidate or if you are conducting a survey, press 9. If you want to speak to someone else in my household, press zero."

Usually the phone call will end before you reach number 4. Please be sure the caller is a telemarketer and not a friend calling to invite you to a holiday party. That could be quite embarrassing.

There are other approaches as well. For example, you could tell the caller he is in big trouble because you are on the Do Not Call List. Or you could ask him to hold on while you diaper the baby.

Members of the Leisure World Chess Club can play chess in the clubhouse without fear of telephone interruption. There was no interruption in the game pictured on the following page. In this game Black can checkmate by moving the Rook to e1. However, it is White's turn to move. What is White's best move? (Note: there are three solutions.)

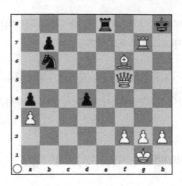

The solution to Puzzle #7 appears on page 247.

So do not wait for the next telephone interruption. Do not wait for a dial tone. Do not wait for Congress to act again. Play chess now!

Columbus, Ferdinand, Isabella, and Chess

October 21, 2014

Compared to other holidays, Columbus Day has not been a commercial success. It just does not generate sales. People do not buy Columbus trees, costumes, decorations, noisemakers or turkeys. Lovers do not exchange sweets. Husbands do not buy flowers for their wives. Let's face it: when is the last time you received a greeting card, wishing you a Happy Columbus Day?

Nevertheless, it is a federal holiday and banks and post offices are closed. First celebrated in New York City on October 12, 1866, it was made into a federal holiday by Franklin D. Roosevelt in 1934. The date was changed to the second Monday in October by legislation signed by Lyndon B. Johnson in 1970--- legislation that set up four other three-day weekends (President's Day, formerly Washington's Birthday; Memorial Day; Labor Day; and Veteran's Day). For retirees, every week has a three-day weekend (and sometimes, even a seven-day weekend).

Many Italian-American communities celebrate the holiday with parades and speeches honoring Christopher Columbus because he was born in Genoa and later discovered what was then called "The New World." Italian-Americans cherish Columbus. He is their hero. He is honored more than Rossini, Michelangelo, or Gina Lollobrigida, none of whom has a holiday of his or her own.

For more than five centuries, Italy did not celebrate Columbus Day. Perhaps Christopher was regarded as a defector inasmuch as he sailed under the Spanish flag. It is rumored that he did not even speak Italian. Since 2004, however, Columbus Day is celebrated in Italy as a national holiday on October 12. Spain celebrates Columbus Day as do many Hispanic countries. It was King Ferdinand and Queen Isabella who financed the Columbus expedition for 16,000 ducats, equivalent to $64,000 (even though dollars had not yet been invented then). Everything was cheaper in those days.

As the story goes, King Ferdinand was preoccupied, playing a chess game with a nobleman (some versions say an archbishop), when Columbus visited Isabella, seeking a title and money for his voyage. Ferdinand was losing the game, but Isabella found that he could win by checkmate in four moves. Ferdinand was delighted to win and, in his euphoric mood, he approved Columbus' request for the title ("Admiral of the Ocean Sea") and finances for the trip. The rest, as they say, is history. Columbus and his crew discovered the Americas (actually an island in the Bahamas) and brought chess to the New World.

Columbus was born in Genoa before Italy became a nation. He believed that one could reach India by sailing to the west of Europe. Many people at the time thought Columbus was crazy because it was common knowledge at the time that the world was flat and that westbound ships would fall off the edge of the earth before they could reach India. The world was not yet ready for global positioning (GPS).

Chess is played in Leisure World on Columbus Day, as in the game shown on the following page. In this game, Black has just moved the Bishop to e6, threatening White's Queen. What is White's best move?

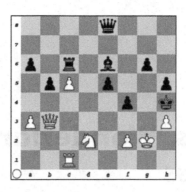

Solution to Puzzle #8 appears on Page 248.

So, do not wait for Columbus Day. Do not wait for another three-day weekend. Do not wait for new world discoveries. Play chess now!

Oil Prices, Wonderland, and Chess

November 4, 2014

It happened while you were on vacation in June. The International Energy Agency reported that the United States had surpassed Saudi Arabia to become the world's largest oil producing country. New technology used in locating and drilling for oil has made this possible. The world is now awash with oil. Prices of crude oil (once higher than $100 per barrel) are coming down sharply (approaching $80) and prices of gasoline at the pump (once reaching $4 per gallon in various states) are sliding down gradually (toward $3 and below).

The Organization of Export Producing Countries (OPEC), the global cartel that raised prices drastically in 1973 through use of the "oil weapon" (a trade embargo) has done nothing to halt the price decline. OPEC members are in disarray. Saudi Arabia and Iran have refrained from cutting production. Russia (now the third leading oil producer) is being hurt more by the drop in oil revenues than by economic sanctions imposed by western nations for Russia's aggression in the Ukraine.

So, where are the trumpets? The parades? The music? Where are the cute majorettes with long legs and short skirts? Why are we not dancing in the streets? Where are the politicians? Where are the speeches? Why is no one taking credit for achieving energy independence? Why is no one proclaiming victory? Mission accomplished?

As Alice discovered in Wonderland, in this world, things aren't always the way they appear to be. High oil prices made it economically feasible to use horizontal drilling and hydraulic fracturing ("fracking") to extract oil in the first place. If oil prices were to decline to a certain level (perhaps below $70 per barrel), it might become necessary to close some wells, thus reducing supplies and hurting the economies of North Dakota and Texas, two leading producers. Although consumers would profit from lower gasoline prices, investors and oil companies would suffer losses in profits and asset values. Pension funds would drop in value.

Also, environmentalists are opposed to fracking which, they claim, contaminates the water supply and makes the ground more susceptible to earthquakes. Politicians do not want to lose the votes of environmentalists and may not be willing to promote higher production levels.

Moreover, many analysts believe that the current price decline is a result of reduced demand in Europe, China, Brazil and India, rather than an oversupply in the market. Lower oil prices are a signal that the world economy is weak. Prices are expected to rise again when economic activity increases. Celebration of energy independence in the USA, therefore, may be premature.

In Wonderland, Alice now might be overheard saying: "Cheap oil makes us yearn for the good old days when prices were higher and times were better."

Unlike tourism, travel and transportation, chess is not sensitive to oil price changes. Games at Leisure World continue regardless of the price level, as in the game illustrated on the following page. In this game, Black has just promoted a Pawn to a Queen and White's King is in a very precarious position. What is White's best move?

[Note: there are two solutions.]

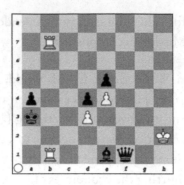

The solution to Puzzle #9 appears on page 248.

So, do not wait for oil prices to drop further! Do not wait for true energy independence! Do not go dancing in the streets! Play chess now!

Is Chess Kosher?

November 18, 2014

The concept of "*kashrut*" (Jewish dietary laws) can be traced back to the Bible (Leviticus, Deuteronomy). Basically, these laws provide that food from unclean animals or unclean creatures of the sea are not safe for consumption. Only food that is marked or labeled with a "*hecksher*" (a certification symbol or stamp of approval) is considered "kosher" or fit for consumption.

The rules are quite extensive. For example, they specify which animals (as well as birds and fowl) may not be eaten and which may be eaten (although some parts of some "clean" animals may not be eaten). The animals which may be eaten must be slaughtered in a certain way before they are fit for consumption. Moreover, meat and dairy products may not be mixed; and utensils used for meat may not be used for dairy and vice versa.

As comprehensive as these rules may be, they do not specifically mention "chess." Somehow chess has been forgotten. It is therefore left to our imaginations to determine whether chess is kosher. Since the dietary laws apply to foods and other products that may come in contact with foods (such as wrappings or utensils), can we assume that the laws do not apply to chess? Or if the chess pieces are edible, do the laws apply? If so, are the black pieces to be considered meat and the white pieces dairy?

In any event, there apparently is no great public outcry for definitive answers to these questions. More appropriate questions, however, may be:

"Under religious law, is it permissible to play chess on the Sabbath?" or "Is it permissible to play chess at all?"

Over the centuries, various religions banned chess in several countries. At one time, playing chess was regarded as practicing idolatry since the carved chess pieces resembled "graven images." About 1400 years ago, chess was played with dice and was banned as a form of gambling. Also, it might have been banned simply because it took time away from prayer.

In religious circles, the question about playing chess on the Sabbath has received some serious attention by rabbis and scholars. The basic answer is that chess can be played on the Sabbath as long as it does not create work. Since writing, tearing, cutting, and the use of electricity may be considered work (or causing others to work), to play chess without violating the Sabbath one must not write down the moves or the scores and must play with another person, not a computer.

Actually the laws of *kashrut* were far ahead of their times. At present, consumer product health and safety laws require certification by government agencies, indicating that foods, cosmetics and other products (baby foods, toys, infant cribs and strollers) are safe for public use. Also, private organizations issue certifications of quality or compliance with standards, such as the Good Housekeeping Seal of Approval, the Underwriters Laboratory Seal, and the American Dental Association Seal of Acceptance. Even used cars can be certified (but not by the Dental Association).

At Leisure World, games are played in the safety and comfort of the clubhouse without regard to government or private certification. As for example, in the game illustrated on the following page, White has just moved the Rook to b8, checking the King. Black has interposed the Queen to block the check. What is White's best move?

[Note: there are two solutions.]

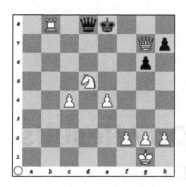

The solution to Puzzle #10 appears on page 248.

So, do not wait for a "*hecksher*." Do not wait for government certification. Do not wait for a seal of approval. Play chess now!

Election Day Results and Chess

December 2, 2014

Once again, the voters have spoken. The mid-term elections are over. The news media have analyzed the results for several weeks so that now we know what the American people want. They want a government that: - - -

- functions, but does not regulate.
- keeps us safe, but does not go to war.
- uses troops only to train foreign soldiers.
- simplifies immigration law so that it can be understood by foreigners.
- does not spend and tax.
- balances the budget without raising taxes.
- takes from the rich and gives to the poor.
- does not redistribute wealth.
- does not interfere with business.
- subsidizes farmers and farm products.
- gives incentives to businesses to create jobs.
- cuts taxes to stimulate the economy.
- can reform the tax code so that it has fewer pages than the Bible.
- shortens and speeds the lines at airports.

The American people want a leader who: ---

- always tells the truth.

- never gets involved in scandals.
- does not leave the country or go on vacation.
- does not fear "fear itself."
- has faith in the American people.
- knows where the buck stops.
- knows where to draw the line in the sand.
- speaks several foreign languages out of both sides of the mouth.
- can negotiate with foreign countries, but not with Congress.
- can use overwhelming military force to our own advantage.
- can make us feel good when the news is bad.
- can sell the Brooklyn Bridge.
- can walk on water.
- can leap tall buildings in a single bound.

The American people are against: ---

- climate change.
- taxes.
- big banks and corporations.
- torture, except for overseas aliens.
- lobbyists and special interests.
- wars that do not defeat our enemies.
- gambling, except in casinos and online.
- illegal immigrants.
- diseases that cross our borders.

The American people want: ---

- clean air, clean water, and free health care.
- free education to the college level.
- quality education without homework, exams, and term papers.
- elimination of academic requirements for college football players.
- postal delivery six days a week when e-mail isn't enough.
- a full TV schedule of highly competitive college football games on Saturdays and pro football on Sundays.
- privacy.

- a chicken in every pot.
- a car in every garage (plus one in the driveway).
- a good five cent cigar.

Once again, the voters were silent on chess. At Leisure World, chess is played without elected officials and without government interference, as in the game illustrated on this page. In this game, Black cannot win, but can hope for a draw by stalemate. It is White's turn to move. What is White's best move?

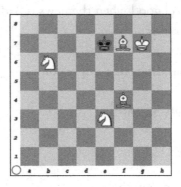

See Solution to Puzzle #11 on page 248.

So, do not wait for the next election. Do not wait for Congress to act. Do not wait for instructions from the American people. Play chess now!

Groundhog Day and Chess

January 23, 2015

Every meteorologist knows that one day each year he or she must compete with a rodent in forecasting the weather. That day is called Groundhog Day. Squirrels and other rodents are not qualified to predict the weather, only groundhogs. Groundhog Day is observed in the United States and Canada on February 2. It is not a legal holiday, but each year the media flock to Punxsutawney, Pennsylvania to report on the event live and to film it for future broadcasts.

Punxsutawney, a town of roughly 6,000 (smaller than the population of Leisure World), is located about 90 miles northeast of Pittsburgh and 100 miles southeast of Erie. (If you live there, you know how to spell it.) The groundhog even has a name: Punxsutawney Phil. If Phil emerges from his hole and sees his shadow, he runs back into his hole, predicting six more weeks of winter. If he comes out and dawdles around, it will be an early spring. This is not easy for groundhogs to do in February, considering that they generally hibernate for the months of October through March. Meteorologists need not worry about the competition since Phil is right only 39 percent of the time, according to Stormfax Weather Almanac.

The event is based on folk lore and has been going on at least since 1887. A growing number of tourists (about 40,000) travel to the town to witness the event and to celebrate. Fans of Punxsutawney Phil hope that February 2 will become a full-fledged holiday some day, with bank and library closings, a paid workday, people decorating their homes with groundhog decorations, wearing groundhog costumes, and giving away candies to children walking the streets.

The Day was given new meaning by the 1993 movie, "Groundhog Day," starring Bill Murray as a weatherman who is trapped in the same day (February 2) and must relive it for years. Some interpreted this to mean that those who do not learn from history are condemned to repeat it. So, every year since 1994, people in the United States and Canada are doomed to watch re-runs of the movie on television in early February.

Contrary to popular belief, the same chess game is not played over and over, not even on Groundhog Day. It is estimated that the number of possible chess games is almost without limit, that is, in the multiples of trillions. In Leisure World, Chess Club players are engaged in unique games each time they play. In the diagram pictured on this page, Black's Queen is in a precarious position in line with the King. White can trap the Queen by moving the Rook to g1. But it is Black's turn to move. What is Black's best move?

The solution to Puzzle #12 appears on Page 248.

So, do not wait for Groundhog Day. Do not wait for Punxsutawney Phil to see his shadow. Do not wait until Groundhog Day becomes a legal holiday. Play chess now!

Will UNESCO Protect Chess?

February 6, 2015

You can rest easily tonight, knowing that an international agency is on the job, protecting historic sites in the United States and elsewhere. It is not the same type of protection as for witnesses who testify against criminals. Under the Witness Protection Program, the witnesses are given new identities and moved to safe places where criminals cannot get to them. This, however, would not be a fitting program for sites of historic interest or natural beauty. After all, you would not want to move the Grand Canyon or the Statue of Liberty and hide them from sightseers. On the contrary, the very purpose of the program is to conserve these sites so that tourists can see them.

The United Nations Educational, Scientific, and Cultural Organization (UNESCO) established a Register of Cultural Heritage Sites based on an international convention adopted in 1972. Since then, 191 nations have ratified the convention and more than 1,000 sites have been listed in about 160 countries. Listing a site on the Register confers official status to the site and presumably protects it against demolition or modification.

UNESCO does not send armed guards to any of the sites to protect them from the threat of economic development, vandalism, graffiti or other desecration; it only provides such sites with an identification number. Apparently, each signatory nation is responsible for upkeep and protection at its sites. Violation of the convention could lead to the ultimate punishment--- removal of the site from the Register (gasp). This has occurred in only two instances thus far.

- In 2007, UNESCO delisted a sanctuary for the Oryx (a rare antelope) because Oman reduced the size of the protected area by 90%, thus destroying its "outstanding universal value."
- In 2009, Germany's Dresden Elbe Valley was removed from the List because a newly built four-lane bridge obstructed the view of the "cultural landscape" and lost its "outstanding universal value as inscribed."

Although the number of possible tangible cultural heritage sites is hardly exhausted, in 2001 UNESCO began a program leading to another official Register--- a List of Intangible Cultural Heritage of Humanity. Included on the List are such intangibles as the gastronomic meal of the French (a customary practice of celebrating weddings, births, anniversaries, accomplishments, etc.). Mexican cuisine (combining culinary techniques and ancestral community customs), and the Argentine tango (music, dance and poetry used in celebrations of national heritage).

If French and Mexican food and Argentina's tango are listed, can chess be far behind? You will be encouraged to know that the European Chess Union (ECU), an organization headquartered in Belgrade, Serbia, has agreed to work with UNESCO experts toward possible recognition of chess as an intangible cultural heritage.

The United States may not be of much help in this regard as it is currently withholding its annual dues because of UNESCO's approval of full membership in the organization for Palestine, without waiting for negotiation of a two-state solution for recognition of a Palestinian state. After two years of non-payment, the United States lost its right to vote at UNESCO general assemblies. The USA is the largest financial contributor to UNESCO, having previously paid about $70 million or 22 percent of the organization's annual budget.

At the Leisure World Chess Club, games continue despite the lack of international recognition and protection, as in the game pictured on the following page. In this game, White is poised to win by moving the Queen to g7 (checkmate!), but it is Black's turn to move. What is Black's best move?

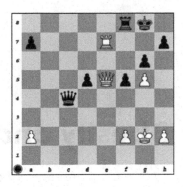

The solution to Puzzle #13 appears on page 248.

So, do not wait for cultural recognition. Do not wait for a vote. Do not wait for international action. Play chess now!

Elephant Obesity and Chess

February 20, 2015

Nobody is more concerned about elephant obesity than the elephants themselves. Obese elephants are ashamed of their appearance. They are self-conscious. Some are depressed. They walk around in circles or rectangles or other geometric patterns.

What would you expect of such massive creatures, the largest living terrestrial animals, with gigantic appetites--- capable of eating 300 pounds of food per day (according to National Geographic)? They spend two-thirds of their day feeding on brush, grasses, leaves, low woody plants, fruits, and tree roots.

Experts estimate that 40 percent of elephants in captivity are obese. The incidence of obesity in elephants living in the wild is not known. This is understandable. First of all, it is a horrendous task to collect all the elephants living outside of captivity and bring them to weigh stations. Then it is extremely difficult to get them to stand on scales without breaking them. Even when the weight is known, it is difficult to determine that an elephant is obese. Fat must be distinguished from muscle, for example. Thus, the study of obesity in elephants is limited largely to those confined in zoos.

Elephants are an endangered species due to loss of habitat resulting from human population expansion and economic development, as well as from poachers who slaughter them for their ivory tusks, meat and hides.

Most elephants (about 420,000) live in Africa; the rest (about 32,000) live in Asia. African elephants generally are larger than Asian elephants, standing as tall as 13 feet and weighing as much as 15,000 pounds; Asian elephants generally are not taller than 11 feet and weigh not more than 11,000 pounds. In both cases, males are larger than females. Asian elephants have smaller ears and only one "finger" in the upper lip of their trunks. African elephants have a second on the lower lip.

In some places Asian elephants are worshipped, particularly in India where they are considered sacred and treated as gods by Hindus (who comprise 80 percent of the population). Buddhists believe the rare white elephants are sacred.

In India's human population, obesity exists alongside poverty and hunger. Apparently, the middle class is growing in weight as well as in number. Rising incomes have brought new food choices to many in the middle class who have become fond of hamburgers and junk food. Five percent of the country's population is obese, according to *The Hindu*, an Indian publication. Weight-loss surgery is becoming popular--- with 18,000 bariatric surgeries performed in India last year at an average cost of $5,000.

But what is to be done with obese elephants in captivity? Certainly, surgery is not the answer--- even for middle-class elephants. More exercise and more activity are probably the best approach. An occasional stampede might be helpful. In some countries, elephants are used for logging and for transportation. (Imagine the reaction of an Uber customer when an elephant shows up at his front door instead of a taxi.) Elephants also could star in Hollywood films. (Remember Dumbo?) Elephants also parade, dance, and do tricks in the circus.

As intelligent creatures who never forget, elephants would make great chess players. If they play chess regularly, it would mean they are not eating food for at least an hour or two per day while they concentrate on their chess moves.

Chess players at the Leisure World Chess Club also forgo eating during games. In the game pictured on this page, it is White's turn to move. What is White's best move?

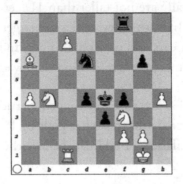

The solution for Puzzle #14 appears on page 248.

So do not wait for an instant cure for obesity. Do not wait for an elephant parade. Do not wait for an elephant to forget. Play chess now!

Love of Country and Chess

March 20, 2015

You may not agree with former New York Mayor Rudy Giuliani that President Obama does not love this country enough, but it is worth noting that patriotism is not a legal requirement for the presidency. You only have to be born in the United States, be over 35 years old, and live within the United States for 14 years to be eligible. Apparently, the unwritten requirements of race, religion, and gender no longer matter so much (although we have not yet had a non-Christian or female president).

At this point in history, perhaps it may be appropriate to institute a test of patriotism as a requirement. Here are some sample questions:

- First thing each morning, do you read the Constitution?
- Do you own a U.S. flag?
- Do you display a U.S. flag at your home on holidays?
- Do you wear a U.S.-flag pin on your lapel daily?
- Do you sing the national anthem at the beginning of sports events?
- Do you buy merchandise made outside the country?

In other countries, of course, the test would be different. In Russia, for example, the following questions might be asked:

- Do you speak Russian?
- Do you drink vodka?

- Do you visit Lenin's tomb often?
- Do you own a dacha?
- Is Dostoevsky your favorite author?
- Do you own a professional basketball team in a foreign country?

In a sense, there is a link between patriotism and chess. International chess tournaments are generally organized according to national teams. Oddly enough, there appears to be some controversy over this.

Many believe that players thrive on the excitement of belonging to a group and representing their country. A national team gives identity to a group of players and stimulates interest of observers and chess fans. Others believe that chess is a game of high intellectual quality which transcends nationalism and that nationalism denigrates the character of the game.

Over the years, numerous chess champs and aspirants have played for countries other than the country of their birth. Russians have played for France, Poland, Germany, and Denmark. Czechoslovaks and Hungarians have played for Russia. Love of country, obviously, is not a requirement in the formation of chess teams.

Bobby Fischer, the eccentric chess genius, would have flunked the patriotism test. He renounced his citizenship after violating a U.S. ban on travel to Yugoslavia, causing the State Department to revoke his passport. Fischer never returned to the United States. He moved to Iceland where he was accepted as a citizen. He had won the world chess championship there in 1972 in a celebrated match against Boris Spassky of the Soviet Union, which was hailed as a Cold War victory by the Western press. Fischer died in Iceland in 2008 at the age of 64 and was buried there.

You don't need to pass a test or have a valid passport to play chess at Leisure World. Residents play chess as individuals, not as members of national teams, as in the diagram on the following page. In this game, it is White's turn to move. White can mate in three moves. Do you see it?

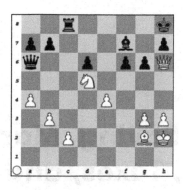

The solution to Puzzle #15 appears on page 248.

So do not wait for a test of patriotism. Do not wait for the national anthem. Do not wait for the fourth of July. Play chess now!

Daylight Saving, March Madness, Taxes, and Chess

April 3, 2015

Have you noticed that Daylight Saving Time (DST) is coming earlier and lasting longer each year? Originally set from the beginning of April to the end of October, DST now runs from March to November or eight months instead of seven.

Some claim this is more evidence of climate change and global warming. They estimate that by the year 2050, the earth will be bathing in sunlight and that we will need to start a program for darkness saving so everyone will know when to go to bed.

They are mistaken. DST is not a worldwide phenomenon. In the United States, it is a creature of the Congress. The most recent legislation is the Energy Policy Act of 2005. Yes, it is political after all. Science and the environment have little to do with it.

One purpose of extending DST to November is to make Halloween Trick-or-Treat safer for children during daylight hours. Who knew that children have a strong lobby in Washington? (And you thought Halloween is supposed to be dark and scary.)

Along with DST, strange things happen in March, including 60-degree days at the end of winter and snowfall on the first day of spring. Also included is a national college basketball tournament, affectionately known as "March

Madness." Sixty-four teams are selected by a committee (sixty-eight if the "play-on" teams are included) to play in an elimination tournament held in numerous cities over the last two weeks of March. One loss and the team is out. The teams that are left (the winners) continue to play as the group gets smaller (to "the sweet sixteen," the elite eight," and the "final four") This year the final games extend into April.

There is no lack of arenas in the country, seating 15-20,000 people each. Many of these indoor arenas are empty during most of the year, waiting for basketball or hockey games, concerts or "special events." During March Madness, however, fans scramble for available seats and pay exorbitant prices to be present at tournament games.

During this period, television is filled with basketball games. Newspapers print schedules of the entire series of games, which are called "brackets." Millions of basketball fans try to pick the winners of all 67 games, filling in the brackets in the newspaper charts. As games are won and lost, checking these brackets becomes a mania, hence "March Madness." People become highly frustrated when their picks become losers, especially when the presumably weaker teams ("the underdogs") beat the favored teams ("the overdogs").

One complication is that the tournament occurs during tax season (or "refund season," as advertised nationally by a leading tax preparation firm.) Thus, it takes time away from tax preparation. One distraught fan is known to have ripped up his tax forms and mistakenly mailed his "bracket" forms to the Internal Revenue Service (IRS). Don't let that happen to you.

In Leisure World, chess is played in the comfort of indoor lighting, heating and air conditioning, irrespective of ongoing tournaments in other sports, even in March. In the game pictured on the following page, White is threatening to capture Black's Rook at e2 and check Black's King with the Rook at g1. It is Black's turn to move. What is Black's best move?

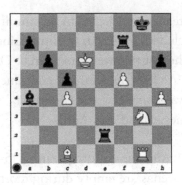

The solution to Puzzle #16 appears on page 249.

So, do not wait for the Final Four. Do not wait for Halloween. Do not wait for "Darkness Saving Time." Play chess now!

Beards, Taxes and Chess

April 17, 2015

Although the Internal Revenue Service (IRS) collects about $3 trillion annually, there is always a search for additional sources of revenue. Taxes are ripe for reform and there is a need for other types of taxes to take the sting out of high taxes on personal and corporate incomes.

This brings to mind the tax on beards, originally imposed in England by King Henry VIII in 1535 and in Russia by Peter the Great in 1698. In many countries beards are regarded as an indication of dignity, wisdom and age. Beards apparently are becoming more popular in the United States in recent years. Unfortunately, the Census of 2010 neglected to count the number of bearded men in the country, making it difficult to estimate the revenue that could be generated by such a tax.

In England and Russia, the beard tax evidently was based on social status. In Russia, for example, a nobleman would be charged 100 rubles annually to maintain a beard (an enormous sum of money at the time), whereas a beggar might only be charged two kopeks. (A copper coin was issued at the time of payment as proof that the tax had been paid. One side of the coin stated (in Russian of course) that the tax had been paid; the other side stated that keeping a beard is a useless burden. Today those coins are valuable collectors' items.)

In Russia, the beard tax was part of Czar Peter's program to modernize, industrialize, and Westernize the country. Only priests and rural peasants were exempt from the tax (although bearded peasants would be charged a

51

ruble or so to enter cities). At the time, the tax was a cultural shock for the clergy, who considered shaving to be a sin. The tax remained in effect for nearly three-quarters of a century before being abolished in 1772.

A beard tax might be too simple to be adapted into the complex tax system of the United States--- a tax code which exceeds 74,000 pages (more than 50 times the size of the bible by page count).

One can visualize, for example, the need for a definition of "beard" to distinguish it from facial hair. Perhaps to qualify as a beard the hair at the point of the chin would have to be at least one-quarter inch in length. Also, after publishing the proposal and allowing a 30-day public comment period, IRS might react by establishing specific provisions and exemptions.

The tax would apply only to men and the bearded lady in the circus. However, there would be no discrimination by hair color, age, or length of beard.

Exemptions could apply to:

- those who are forbidden to shave because of religion;
- those who cannot shave because of medical reasons; and
- baseball players and other professional athletes

Reduced rates could apply to:

- beards trimmed by barbers certified by the IRS;
- beards trimmed at home with products made by U.S. manufacturers making large political contributions; and
- beards trimmed by foreign barbers whose governments have tax treaties with the United States to avoid double taxation.

And how would IRS enforce the tax? Thousands of men could shave off their beards on April 14 and grow them back the rest of the year. Perhaps it would be easier to tax baldness.

At Leisure World, chess playing is not taxed. Chess can be played with or without beards. In the game illustrated on this page, Black's King is in trouble, but does White have enough power to win now? It is White's turn to move. What is White's best move?

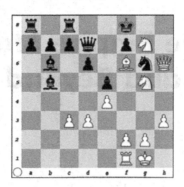

The solution to Puzzle #17 appears on page 249.

So, do not wait for tax reform. Do not wait for a Census on beards. Do not wait for beards to grow to taxable lengths. Play chess now!

Chess, the Empire State Building and Beyond

May 8, 2015

To emphasize the size of an object and impress an audience, speakers often compare the object to a famous building (especially the Empire State Building). Thus, you will find that---

- New York City throws out enough garbage each day to fill the Empire State Building.
- Americans use about 30 billion cardboard boxes a year, enough to make a pile as big as a football field and as high as the World Trade Center in New York.
- Some new container ships are longer than the height of the Empire State Building. France's Eiffel Tower can fit inside some container ships.
- To expand the Panama Canal, crews will dredge 130 million cubic meters of rock and soil, enough to fill the Empire State Building 130 times. Walls of the new canal will have enough steel to build 18 Eiffel Towers.
- If laid on end, the Commerce Building in Washington, DC would come within 200 feet of equaling the height of the Empire State Building.
- Enough hazardous waste is generated in one year to fill the New Orleans Superdome 1,500 times over.

Another way to explain the significance of an object is to compare it to the distance between the earth and the moon, or the distance around the equator. Thus, you will find that---

- Every year we fill enough garbage trucks to form a line that would stretch from the earth, halfway to the moon.
- The aluminum cans recycled in the United States since 1972 placed end to end could stretch to the moon some 170 times.
- Every day, the heart creates enough energy to drive a truck 20 miles, equivalent to driving to the moon and back over a lifetime.
- If you stretched the DNA in all 10 trillion cells in your body from end to end, they would reach the moon and back almost 1500 times (or four times to the sun and back).
- If you lined up all the polystyrene foam cups made in just one day, they would circle the earth.
- If the blood vessels of an adult were lined up end to end, they would circle the equator four times.
- On average people walk around 70,000 miles in their life, which calculates to nearly three times around the equator.
- Americans discard 4 million tons of office paper every year, enough to build a 12 foot-high wall of paper from New York to California.

All of this reminds us of George Bernard Shaw's famous quotation that if all economists were laid end to end, they would never reach a conclusion.

We have no idea what could be reached if all chess players were laid end to end, but this would make for an interesting discussion.

In Leisure World, chess is played face to face. There is no objective of reaching a particular destination at any particular time. Games are played simply for the intellectual enjoyment of them. In the game pictured on the following page, it is White's turn to move. Can White force a victory in three moves?

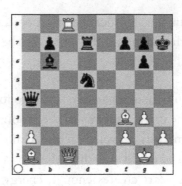

Solution to Puzzle #18 appears on page 249.

So do not wait for chess players to fill the Empire State Building. Do not wait for chess players to reach the moon or circle the equator. Do not wait for a wall of paper. Play chess now!

The Congress of Vienna and Chess

May 22, 2015

If an event starts in one year and ends in the next, when should the anniversary be celebrated? The Congress of Vienna started in November 1814 and ended in September 1815. Should the bicentennial anniversary of the event be celebrated in 2014 or 2015? Those clever Austrian businessmen had the perfect solution: celebrate in both years.

Dutch businessmen went one step further; they are celebrating for three years. That is because Prince Wilhelm (later King Wilhelm I) landed on a beach in the Netherlands in 1813 after his father had fled from the French to England in 1795. Then the Congress of Vienna created the Kingdom of the Netherlands, which at the time included Belgium and Luxembourg. So, the Netherlands and its Caribbean territories: Curacao, Aruba, and St. Maarten are currently celebrating the Kingdom's 200th birthday.

The Congress of Vienna of 1815 truly is a historic event. It is remarkable for a number of reasons. Some regard it as the forerunner of the League of Nations or the United Nations (although it included only European jurisdictions, about 200 in all). It restored world order to pre-Napoleonic days, set the boundaries between countries, and established an extended period of European peace. No major wars occurred for nearly one hundred years following the Congress. Sadly, though, celebration of the 100th anniversary was marred by the outbreak of World War I, the war to end all wars.

In addition to being a significant international diplomatic event, the Congress was a great accomplishment from a logistical standpoint. Overall, the event reportedly brought around 100,000 people from various parts of Europe to the Austrian capital, swelling its population by about a third (at least temporarily). Organizing and conducting such a huge conference must have been considered an enormous feat in the days prior to air travel, railroads, five-star hotels, telephones, taxis, electrification, and indoor plumbing.

Imagine the supplies needed to transport thousands of delegates, officials, and others to the city and to house them. Horses needed stables, food, water and horseshoe repairs. People needed food, water, beer, and wine at a time when electric refrigeration and frozen foods did not yet exist.

Negotiations with hundreds of entities would have been extremely difficult. This, however, was simplified with five countries taking major responsibility: Russia, Prussia, Austria, and Britain (the victors) and France (the vanquished). Germany and Italy then consisted mainly of city-states, which would not become unified nations until the 1870's.

What did representatives from the other 195 jurisdictions do while the negotiations were going on? Entertainment consisted of parades, military reviews, concerts, and theater. Ludwig van Beethoven conducted his Seventh Symphony at one of the concerts and composed a cantata specifically for the occasion. Many receptions and balls were held and Strauss waltzes, originally considered naughty and indecent, were becoming fashionable. Royalty and the upper classes seemed to be having a grand old time.

Negotiations took eleven months to complete. Progress was slow, prompting the famous quotation: "Le congres danse beaucoup, mais il ne marche pas" ("The congress dances, but does not progress").

In addition to the many forms of entertainment during the Congress, perhaps there was time for chess too. This is not easily verifiable though.

At Leisure World, there is always time for chess, as in the diagram pictured on the following page. In this game, Black has just made a daring move by capturing a Pawn at h3 and threatening checkmate on the next move. It is White's turn to move. What is White's best move?

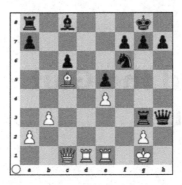

The solution to Puzzle #19 appears on page 249.

So, do not wait for a large international conference. Do not wait for a horse drawn carriage or an invitation to the dance. Do not wait for revival of the monarchy. Play chess now!

Chess and the Glut
of Nations

June 5, 2015

There are too many nations in the world. Founded by 51 nations in 1945, the United Nations membership has grown to 193. Since then, 75 new nations have achieved independence. Many are former colonies of European powers in Africa and Asia. Africa alone now has more than 50 countries. In addition, 15 countries emerged from the former Soviet Union and 7 from Yugoslavia.

This has created problems for border control officials, who must verify the authenticity of foreign passports, and for international travelers, who must wait in long lines while this is done. Also, public and private transportation near UN headquarters in New York are often stuck in massive traffic jams along First Avenue between 42nd and 48th Streets. Moreover, the proliferation of nations has made the Olympic Parade much longer and more boring than necessary. At the Winter Games in Sochi, Russia in 2014, for example, athletes from 88 countries marched seemingly for hours, in alphabetical order of their country names in Russian.

Think of all the duplication of government bureaucracies, multiplicity of armies, and excessive management and staffing. The proliferation of differing policies leads to greater competition, conflicts of interest, wars, inefficiencies in distribution of food and resources, a surplus of national anthems, and far too many statistics.

This is not an accident. The League of Nations and the United Nations both adopted programs to prepare former colonies for self-governance, recognizing that "the interests of the inhabitants are paramount." All of this is for the sake of promoting good neighborliness, international peace and security.

To be eligible for recognition as a nation, an area may need a permanent population, a defined territory, a government, and the capacity to enter into relations with other areas. Other than that, there are little or no criteria to qualify as a nation. There are no requirements based on geographic location, area, population, history, language or religion. Much depends simply on diplomatic recognition by at least one UN member country.

Thus, a nation may be as small as Andorra with a population of 80,000 and an area of 200 square miles, or as large as China. It can be an island like Singapore or a landlocked country, such as Bolivia. It can have 387 languages like India, or two like Canada. Some countries are recognized only by a small number of others. For example, the State of Israel is not recognized by 32 UN member countries. The Republic of Abkhazia is recognized only by 6 UN member states. Taiwan (Republic of China) is recognized by 21 UN member nations. Separatists in Scotland, Spain, and elsewhere aspire to become independent nations.

How can we rid the world of meaningless national allegiances? To reorganize the world into a smaller number of countries would be a Herculean task. Is it feasible to change or eliminate boundaries? Should limits be placed on the total number of nations? Or on the number of countries that can be recognized each year? Should colonization be restored? Or should we look to the business community to help arrange rational mergers and acquisitions between large countries with smaller countries?

In Leisure World, the Chess Club has no boundaries. There are no aspirations for international recognition. Its objective is simply to provide mental stimulation and entertainment for its members, as in the game pictured on the following page. Black has just moved the Queen to f2, threatening to capture White's Rook at e1. It is White's turn to move. What is White's best move?

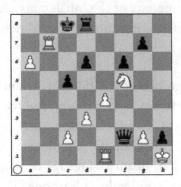

The solution to Puzzle #20 appears on page 249.

So, do not wait for consolidation of surplus nations. Do not wait for the return of colonization. Do not wait for genuine international peace and security. Play chess now!

Fourth of July and Chess

July 3, 2015

By now, it is common knowledge that we celebrate July fourth on the wrong date. In a euphoric mood upon completion of the Declaration of Independence, John Adams (a signer of the Declaration and second President of the United States) wrote a letter to his wife, Abigail, stating that "The second day of July, 1776, will be the most memorable epoch in the history of America. I am apt to believe that it will be celebrated by succeeding generations as the great anniversary festival. It ought to be commemorated as the day of deliverance ... solemnized with pomp and parade, with shows, games, sports, guns, bells, bonfires, and illuminations, from one end of this continent to the other, from this time forward forever more."

The Declaration was adopted by the Continental Congress on July 4, 1776. July 4th is what we celebrate. Most of the delegates actually signed the Declaration on August 2. The last delegate to sign, according to the National Archives, is believed to be Thomas McKean of Delaware, sometime in 1777. Because the Internet had not yet been invented, the British government in London did not learn that the United States had declared independence until August 30. Independence was not acknowledged by Britain until the Treaty of Paris in 1783. The United States itself did not recognize July 4th as a legal paid federal holiday until 1938.

Today, July fourth is observed with cookouts, grilled hot dogs, parades, concerts, and fireworks. More hot dogs are consumed on July 4th than on any other day of the year--- about 150 million pounds. More than $300 million worth of flags, banners and emblems are sold. More than $200 million pounds of fireworks are exploded. John Adams would have been impressed and delighted. (Note that Adams envisioned "illuminations" in these celebrations, not necessarily fireworks.)

July 4th concerts generally conclude with the rousing and triumphant Overture of 1812, accompanied by the firing of cannons and explosion of fireworks overhead. The Overture (which has nothing to do with the War of 1812) was written in 1882 by a Russian, who personally thought it was without artistic merit because it was too loud and noisy and lacked warmth and feeling. Nevertheless, the composer, Peter Ilyich Tchaikowsky, then 50 years old, conducted the 1812 Overture at the grand opening of Carnegie Hall on May 5, 1891 (Yes, Cinco de Mayo).

There is conflicting information on whether or not John Adams played chess, but his son John Quincy Adams did play chess. Also, Jefferson, Madison, and Monroe were ardent chess players, as was Benjamin Franklin. It seems almost patriotic, therefore, to play chess on July 4th (Cuatro de Julio). Some places, in fact, conduct annual chess tournaments on July 4th (New Jersey, for example).

At Clubhouse II in Leisure World, chess is played without speeches and celebratory fanfare all year round. In the game shown on this page, Black is in trouble, particularly with the Queen defending the King and the Pawn at e6 vulnerable to attack by White's Rook at e1. What is White's best move?

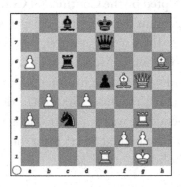

Solution to Puzzle #21 appears on page 249.

So, do not wait for a parade. Do not wait for patriotic music. Do not wait for fireworks. Play chess now!

Why Chess Is Better than Baseball

July 17, 2015

It is a big disappointment to learn that Abner Doubleday did not invent baseball. It is a myth. Why weren't we notified sooner? Is nothing more sacred in America than baseball, the national pastime?

We should have been more suspicious in 1907, when A. J. Spalding organized a commission to report on the origin of the sport. Spalding was a former star pitcher who had become a sporting goods manufacturer. Doubleday, a career U.S. Army officer and a Union General during the American Civil War, was not available to testify before the panel as he had died in 1893. He had never claimed to be the inventor of baseball. On the basis of some questionable evidence, however, Spalding's panel found that Doubleday, as a young man, had invented and played the game in Cooperstown, New York in 1839, named the sport "baseball," and developed the rules. No written records have ever been found to corroborate these claims. Yet, on the basis of the report, businessmen and major league officials established the National Baseball Hall of Fame and Museum in Cooperstown in the 1930s.

It was a story Americans wanted to believe--- that a young man in the cow pasture of a quaint rural town invented the game and later became a Civil War hero. Doubleday participated in the opening battle of the war--- some say he fired the first shot in defense of Fort Sumter--- and played a pivotal role in the early fighting at the Battle of Gettysburg--- where a monument now stands in his honor.

Cooperstown, meanwhile, capitalized on its reputation as the birthplace of baseball. A celebration of baseball's hundredth anniversary attracted 10,000 visitors to the town of 2,800 and featured the appearance of some of baseball's greatest stars, such as Babe Ruth and Cy Young. A one-room museum at the time, the National Baseball Hall of Fame opened officially and baseball's great legends from the past played an exhibition game at nearby Doubleday Field, built on the precise spot where the game was supposedly invented a century before.

An English-born baseball journalist, Henry Chadwick, who was a member of Spalding's panel, wrote a dissenting opinion, contending that baseball originated from two English games: rounders and cricket. A book published in 1947 by historian Robert Henderson on the history of bat and ball games, debunked the myth of Cooperstown, documenting baseball's older origins linked to games played in England.

Perhaps, as stated by Jeff Idelson of the Baseball Hall of Fame, "Baseball wasn't really born anywhere… meaning that the evolution of the game was long and continuous and has no clear, identifiable single origin."

Chess enthusiasts will tell you that chess is better than baseball because:

- it has a longer history;
- it is played in more countries than baseball;
- it is played by more people than baseball;
- in chess there is no advantage due to height, weight, gender, or age;
- it is easier to play (no need for acres of land, large stadiums);
- it can be played without uniforms, baseballs, bats, and gloves;
- you do not need 18 people to play a game of chess;
- it can be played year-round regardless of the weather;
- you do not need to wear a beard to play chess;
- there are no lucky bounces in chess;
- baseball has too many statistics;

- chess players are less prone to injury; and
- umpires are not needed to decide if you made a good move.

In Leisure World, baseball is not played as often as chess. In a recent chess game, pictured on this page, it is Black's turn to move. Can Black prevent White from queening (promoting a Pawn to Queen by reaching the eighth row) and win the game?

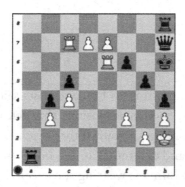

Solution to Puzzle #22 appears on page 250.

So, do not wait for the umpire to cry "Play Ball". Do not wait for the seventh inning stretch. Do not wait for Pete Rose to be inducted into the Baseball Hall of Fame. Play chess now!

August: No Holiday for Chess

August 7, 2015

Don't look now, but the sun is on fire. Scientists know because they can detect sun storms and sudden explosions that release flares into space, traveling at millions of miles an hour. If they reach Earth, sun flares pose a danger to power grids and communications, but these streams of magnetic energy are harmless to humans wearing sunscreen.

August is that kind of a month--- a hot, sunny month--- a time for immersing oneself in water at beaches and swimming pools to cool down one's body and to apply lotions to protect against the sun. It is a slow month, a month of vacations. Nearly everybody is on vacation. In European countries, governments close down for the full month. In Rome, it is said, the local population goes elsewhere and leaves the city entirely to tourists.

There are no major national holidays to celebrate in August. You may have heard that there are a number of celebrations during August, such as Friendship Day, Women's Equality Day, National Catfish Month, National Water Quality Month, Peach Month, and National Immunization Awareness Month. These have very little economic or psychological impact on people and August is just too hot for Halloween costumes, Valentine candies, Easter eggs and Santa Claus. It is too hot for heavy work or even heavy thinking.

From the beginning August was an underprivileged month. Under the Roman calendar, it had only 29 days. (Tsk. Tsk.) Originally, it was called Sextilis because it was the sixth month of the year. It became the eighth month after January and February were added to the calendar. When Julius Caesar created the Julian calendar in 45 BC, two days were added giving the month 31 days. Later, it was renamed Augustus in honor of the first emperor of Rome, Caesar Augustus.

Those who believe nothing ever happens in August should be aware of some of the following events:

- in baseball, Lou Gehrig hit his 23rd career grand slam (1928); and Babe Ruth hit his 600th home run (1931);
- the Beatles made their last appearance at the Cavern Club in Liverpool (1963);
- in London, half the audience walked out during a play by Samuel Beckett, "Waiting for Godot," (1955);
- Jesse Owens won the first of his four Olympic medals in Berlin (1936);
- the Indianapolis 500 race track opened (1909);
- Leonard Bernstein conducted his last concert at Tanglewood, Massachusetts (1990);
- the Mona Lisa painting was stolen by a worker at the Louvre Museum (1911);
- the world's first motorcycle was patented by Gottlieb Daimler (1885);
- the first U.S. Census was conducted (1790);
- the world's first underground railway opened in London (1870);
- Wild Bill Hickok was killed while playing poker (1876);
- the first electric traffic light was installed in Cleveland, Ohio (1914);
- Gertrude Ederle became the first woman to swim the English Channel (1926);
- Magician Harry Houdini survived 91 minutes in a coffin submerged in a swimming pool (1926);
- Theodore Roosevelt became the first U.S. President to ride in a car (1902);
- Amelia Earhart became the first woman to fly across the United States non-stop (1932);

- Mars made its closest approach to Earth in nearly 60,000 years (2003);
- Caleb Bradham renamed his carbonated beverage "Pepsi Cola" (1898); and
- Mark Spitz won the first of seven Olympic medals for swimming (1972).

All these events occurred in August, along with the sailing of Christopher Columbus to find a western route to India (1492); the burning of the White House by British troops (1814); the beginning of World War I (1914); and dropping of the atomic bomb and the surrender of Japan to end World War II (1945).

Unperturbed by the heat and lack of national holidays, chess continues in Leisure World without interruption in August. Chess is played regularly in the air conditioned comfort of Clubhouse II, as evidenced in the diagram on tis page. It is White's turn to move. What is White's best move?

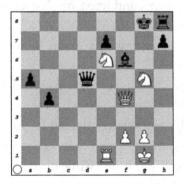

The solution to Puzzle# 23 appears on page 250.

So, do not wait for a cool month. Do not wait for a major holiday. Do not wait for a great new event. Play chess now!

Cuba Plays Chess

August 21, 2015

In 1950, Senator Joseph McCarthy warned that Communists had infiltrated the State Department. What would he have said now that we have recognized China and severed relations with Taiwan (in 1979) and recognized the Russian Federation as successor to the Soviet Union (in 1991)? What would he have said about the current process of restoring relations with Communist Cuba?

Since the Cuban missile crisis of February 1962, the United States has maintained an economic embargo against this island nation of 11 million people, whose government is a one-party dictatorship with totalitarian control of the economy and society--- a government that represses civil liberties.

Senator McCarthy has not lived through the last five decades in which the world is changing and Communism itself is changing. In fact, some now call the economic system in Russia and China "state capitalism" or "market socialism." Perhaps, even Senator McCarthy would have changed by this time.

President Obama has said that "we don't have to be imprisoned by the past." He also said, "When something isn't working, we can and should change" and he reportedly shook hands with Cuban President Raúl Castro at a recent summit meeting in Panama. Heavens!

The latest chapter in this saga is the agreement to open (or re-open) embassies in each country. Is it possible that it will be difficult to staff these embassies because of travel bans that still exist in each country? In the United States, the removal of economic sanctions requires an act of Congress.

In case you were not aware, Cuba is "chess country." Despite its small size, it is ranked 7th or 8th in the world by the International Chess Federation (FIDE). It has one of the strongest chess-playing cultures, dating back to the days of Christopher Columbus. Not only is chess taught in the school system, it is compulsory and is taught at all levels of education, including college. The training of chess professors, which began in 2003, has produced around 1,000 professors.

The first Cuban championship tournament was held in 1860. Cuba reveres its chess champions, particularly Raul Capablanca who held the world title from 1921-27. A chess club in Havana is named after him and a Capablanca Memorial Tournament is held each year. Cuba has hosted three world championship matches.

During evening hours in Havana, chess games can be seen on the streets under lamppost lights. Cuba has even created postage stamps with chess themes. Four of the seven stamps portrayed a drawing of Capablanca; others pictured a chessboard and chess knights.

Famous U.S. chess player Bobby Fischer competed in the 4th Capablanca Memorial in 1965 by telex from the Marshall Chess Club in New York after being denied a visa by the State Department to compete in person. Fischer's application to visit Cuba as a journalist for the Saturday Review and Chess Life was rejected by passport officials because they did not think a chess tournament was a valid reason to visit a Communist country and because they did not believe Fischer was a bona fide journalist.

In 1966, however, Fischer was allowed to compete in the 17th FIDE Chess Olympiad in Havana. Cuba spent over $5 million on that event. Fidel Castro played several exhibition games including a draw with Grandmaster

Tigran Petrosian and a win against Bobby Fischer, according to a history written by Bill Wall of chess.com.

Chess transcends politics. At Leisure World, residents do not need a visa to play chess, nor do they need evidence of chess education in public or private schools. In the game pictured on this page, Black's King is exposed and Black's Queen is under attack by White's Rook at h5. However, it is Black's turn to move. What is Black's best move?

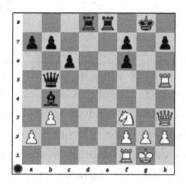

The solution to Puzzle# 24 appears on page 250.

So, do not wait for Senator McCarthy's advice! Do not wait for the end of sanctions against Cuba! Do not wait for capitalism to return to Cuba! Play chess now!

Is Chess 'Good as Gold'?

September 4, 2015

Something is wrong with the price of gold. It is going down, not up. That is historically incorrect. During times of economic uncertainty and political unrest, people want to hold something tangible, like gold, not paper money. And these are uncertain times. Greece is bankrupt. Italy, Spain, and Portugal are deeply in debt. Even the economies of the United States and Germany are sluggish. China's rapid growth has also slowed down and China has devalued its currency. Terrorism and wars are raging in the Middle East.

Gold has intrinsic value and has been regarded as a preserver of purchasing power that has held its value for over 5,000 years. Recently, however, the price has been slipping. It reached a peak of about $1,900 an ounce in 2012, but has since declined to nearly $1,000 (at the time of this writing). At least one study expects the price to drop even further (perhaps to $350 an ounce). What is happening? Gold-holding almost always has been used as a means of protecting the value of one's assets. People who distrust the value of paper money are known to have stored gold in their mattresses. Have they suddenly lost faith in gold? Have their mattresses become too lumpy?

When is the last time you bought an ounce of gold? (Hmm.) No wonder the price is falling.

For many years, Americans were not allowed to own gold. During the Great Depression, Franklin D. Roosevelt issued a proclamation to stem the outflow of gold from the Treasury. Accordingly, exports of gold were prohibited and the Treasury and other financial institutions were not permitted to convert currency and deposits into gold coins and ingots. Individuals were not permitted to hold or trade in gold and were required to cash their gold into dollars. The prohibition on gold-holding ended in 1974 when President Gerald Ford rescinded the 1934 proclamation.

In 1973, President Richard Nixon suspended convertibility of the dollar into gold, in effect ending the international gold standard, allowing exchange rates to float.

The price of gold is usually expressed in troy ounces, which are heavier than regular (avoirdupois) ounces. It only takes 12 ounces to make a pound, not 16. (Troy Ounce. Sounds like the name of a comic strip character, or a young rock star, or the heroin's new lover in a TV soap opera.) When governments or central banks buy gold, however, the quantity is expressed in metric tons, not ounces. One metric ton equals 32,150.7466 troy ounces. Remember that for your next purchase.

Reportedly, more than 60 percent of all global central bank reserves are held in dollars, not gold. (Aren't these the same banks that are printing new paper money to relieve the economic recession that began in 2008, the monetary policy known as "quantitative easing"?) Historically, gold has been held as a hedge against inflation. Currently, however, despite the increase in paper money supply, consumer prices generally have been flat or falling and interest rates are near zero. Thus, if there is no inflation, what is the point of buying gold?

As reported by the World Gold Council (a market development organization for the gold industry, headquartered in London), global gold reserves amount to roughly 32,000 metric tons. The United States, the world's leading gold-holding country, which held over 20,000 tons of gold reserves in 1952, now holds only about 8,000 tons. China, a large buyer of gold, has not bought any recently. Perhaps its bankers are waiting for lower prices to buy larger piles of gold bars with their U.S. dollars. [Note: after this article was written, the price of gold began to rise--- without permission of the author.]

Chess is not as good as gold in the sense that people and governments do not buy chess sets to hedge against inflation or to protect their wealth. Some luxury chess sets are made of gold, however, and are available for as much as $300,000. At the Leisure World Chess Club, the game is usually played with more modest sets made of wood or plastic. It is easier to lift the chess pieces.

In the game pictured on this page, White has just moved the Knight from f3 to d2, uncovering the Bishop, and threatening the Black Queen. Nevertheless, Black can win the game by checkmate in two moves. It is Black's turn to move. How can Black accomplish the checkmate?"

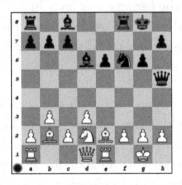

The solution to Puzzle #25 appears on page 250.

So, do not wait for gold prices to rise to $1,900 an ounce. Do not wait for return of the international gold standard. Do not wait for a gold chess set. Play chess now!

Rhino Day and Chess

September 18, 2015

Pity the poor rhinoceros.
The horn on his nose is preposterous.
But like it or not,
That's what he's got.
It distinguishes him from the hippopotamus.

To poachers and practitioners of traditional Chinese medicine, the horn is the most valuable part of the rhino. Hundreds of rhinos are killed each year by poachers who illegally sell the horns on the black market at prices over $100,000 per kilogram--- more than double the price of gold.

Over the past 3,000 years, rhino horn powder in combination with Chinese herbs, have been used to treat infections and to reduce fever. Since 1993, however, rhino horn is completely banned for medical treatment in China, Taiwan and South Korea. Its use there is now permitted only for research to develop substitutes. A huge market, though, has emerged in Vietnam where it is used as a hangover cure and is even promoted as a cure for cancer, although there is no scientific basis for such claims.

Early in the twentieth century, approximately 500,000 rhinos were prevalent in Africa and Asia. However, the recent sharp increase in poaching is driving these animals closer to extinction. Between 1970 and 1987, 85 percent of the world rhino population was killed. The number currently in the wild has been reduced to about 29,000.

Large-scale poaching remains a constant threat and is believed to finance terrorist and criminal activities around the world. Conservationists are trying to come up with solutions. One attempt is embodied in the Convention on International Trade in Endangered Species, an international treaty, which entered into force in July 1975, banning imports of endangered plants and animals into member countries. Although some 180 countries are now members of the Convention, its effectiveness in protecting rhinos from poachers appears to be limited.

One recent proposal calls for dehorning rhinos to make them unattractive and less valuable to poachers. The difficulties and costs in locating all rhinos in the wild and removing their horns are well recognized. (Comment: Not only would this be expensive, but it is basically counterintuitive: subjecting the species to surgery which would radically alter their appearance. It is like "cutting your nose to spite your face.") Also the horns grow back over time. A similar approach is to get genetic engineers to build hornless rhinos. This would take years, of course, and its practicality is questionable.

Another approach under consideration is to legitimize the sale of rhino horn. In South Africa, where the largest number of rhinos is located, private ownership of rhinos is legally permitted. In fact, some 28 per cent of the national rhino herd, around 5,000 rhinos, is held in private ownership. The government of South Africa is said to have tons of rhino horns in reserves and possibly could release them for sale. The association representing rhino owners advocates the legal sale of rhino horns in an open market, to drive prices down so that it would become uneconomic for poachers and smugglers to operate.

Rhinos play a vital role in the ecosystem. Rhinos prune bushes, small trees and shrubs as they eat, and when they defecate, they disperse seeds which eventually germinate and grow, shaping the landscape. Rhinos generally weigh 2-3,000 pounds and produce about 50 pounds of dung per day. Rhinos that defecate in water can indirectly provide nutrients for other species, like fish, which eat their dung. Rhinos mark their territory with dung and urine. They are retromingent animals (they urinate backwards), depositing tons of nutrients from terrestrial African ecosystems into aquatic ones.

You need to know this because World Rhino Day, September 22, is approaching. It is celebrated in 15 countries, including the USA. You can celebrate Rhino Day by visiting a zoo or by wearing a colorful T-shirt with an appropriate slogan, like "Save the Rhino" or "I Heart Babak" (which is "I Love Rhinos" in Indonesian). Show your support for the Rhino. Stand behind them (but not literally; remember they are retromingent).

At Leisure World, you can always stand behind the Chess Club because all the members are thoroughly housebroken. None are retromingent. In the game pictured on this page, it is White's turn to move. White can win in three moves. What are White's best moves?

The solution to Puzzle #26 appears on page 250.

So, do not wait for genetically modified rhinos! Do not wait for rhino extinction! Do not wait for the end of poaching! Play chess now!

Emissions, Statistics and Chess

October 2, 2015

Some of the world's most interesting statistics are about things that haven't happened (and may not ever happen). As everyone knows, statistics paint a picture that helps to give depth and meaning to an otherwise obscure and complex situation or problem. Politicians and bureaucrats often say that once an issue is quantified, it is easier to deal with it.

Probably the most dramatic statistics are generated by the environment and climate change. For example, in current television commercials, the National Association of Manufacturers tells us that new regulations for strengthened air quality standards proposed by the Environmental Protection Agency could cost the average household $830 in lost consumption. Between 2017 and 2040, NAM projects the new regulations would cost the country 1.4 million jobs and $1.7 trillion in foregone economic activity.

Many of the environmental statistics are concerned with the reduction of carbon dioxide emissions. Thus, we read that the U.S. transportation sector (planes, trains, ships, and freight) produces around *thirty percent* of all U.S. global warming emissions. CO_2 emissions from U.S. cars & trucks totaled 314 million metric tons in 2002 (equivalent to emissions released from burning all the coal in a train 50,000 miles long -- enough to circle around the world, twice, according to the Environmental Defense Fund).

Our personal vehicles are a major cause of global warming. Collectively, "cars and trucks account for nearly one-fifth of *all* U.S. emissions, emitting around 24 pounds of carbon dioxide and other global-warming gases for every gallon of gas."

Substituting biking and walking for auto transportation could lead to fuel savings of 3.8 billion gallons a year and reduce greenhouse gas emissions by 33 million tons per year. (This is equivalent to replacing 19 million conventional cars with hybrids, according to Rails-to-Trails Conservancy).

If 5 percent of New Yorkers switched to biking to work instead of commuting by car or taxi, it could save 150 million pounds of CO2 emissions per year, equivalent to the amount reduced by planting a forest 1.3 times the size of Manhattan. Similarly, bicyclists in Philadelphia ride 260,000 miles daily, saving 47,450 tons of CO2 emissions and bicycle traffic in Copenhagen prevents 90,000 tons of CO2 from being emitted annually.

Unnecessary vehicle idling in New York City costs drivers $28 million a year, causes as much smog-forming pollution as 9 million large trucks driving from the Bronx to Staten Island, and wastes the gasoline equal to 40,000 cars driving from Midtown to JFK Airport.

A 10 cent per gallon increase in the gasoline tax, it is said, would reduce carbon emissions from vehicles in the United States by about 1.5 percent.

As much as automobiles and trucks now contribute to air pollution, motor vehicles actually solved an environmental problem in the past century created by horse transportation.

In 1894, the Times of London estimated that by 1950 every street in the city would be buried nine feet deep in horse manure. One prediction in New York in the 1890s foresaw that by 1930 the horse droppings would rise to Manhattan's third-story windows. With each horse producing 15-30 pounds of manure per day and a horse population of about 170,000 in New York City in the 1880s, **some 3-4 million pounds of manure were piling onto city streets each day.**

Health officials in Rochester, New York, calculated in 1900, that the fifteen thousand horses in that city produced enough manure in a year to make a pile 175 feet high covering an acre of ground and breeding sixteen billion flies, each one a potential spreader of germs.

The LW Chess Club is not concerned about horse manure or carbon dioxide emissions. Chess makes no contribution to U.S. air pollution or to environmental statistics. In the game pictured on this page, White has more manpower and is on the verge of winning the game by moving the Queen to a7, but it is Black's turn to move. What is Black's best move?

The solution to Puzzle #27 appears on page 250.

So, do not wait for more environmental statistics! Do not wait for the return of horse transportation! Do not wait for bicycles to replace motor vehicles! Play chess now!

Chess on Mars

October 16, 2015

NASA scientists have found water on Mars again. This time, however, they believe it is flowing--- although they haven't actually seen it flowing, but they have seen signs that it has flowed. Mountains on the planet have crevices which seem to indicate that flowing water has cut through the surface.

For more than three decades, the United States has launched spacecraft to probe the surface of Mars. Cameras and communication equipment are now on the planet and orbiting the planet, sending back information on the soil and atmosphere to determine if life exists there. However, no life has yet been found and without such a discovery, we may never get to know if there is chess on Mars.

The trouble is that the camera on the satellite that orbits the planet only operates at 3 pm Mars time, the water appears only in summer when the temperature is hot enough, and the water evaporates very quickly. The source of the water is not known. Some believe it may have been trapped underground. Others believe it may be a result of deliquescence--- absorbed from the atmosphere.

Based on pictures of the planet, it would seem that Mars is more suitable for skiing than for swimming. World travelers are becoming bored with the sunshine of the Caribbean, the antiquity of Europe and the safaris of Africa. Travel to Mars could prove to be a boon for the tourism industry. The abundance of transit time can be used to play chess and to participate in other forms of entertainment. Security screening can be simplified and expedited and the seat belt safety video can be updated for interplanetary travel. A small gift shop with souvenirs can be placed on board.

NASA discovered ice on Mars in 2002 and found streaks in the terrain in 2010. More recently NASA found a gigantic slab of ice beneath the surface midway between the planet's equator and North Pole, as thick as a thirteen-story building and as large as California and Texas combined. Until now, however, there has been no evidence that the ice has ever liquefied. So this is an important discovery. If there is liquid water on Mars, the planet may be able to sustain life.

The water is also said to be briny, although nobody has actually tasted it yet. Even if the water is undrinkable, at least you can do your laundry there.

To find out more about these mysteries, we may have to wait until NASA's next space probe (manned or unmanned) arrives on Mars in 2020. In the meantime, world travelers can get a preview of a visit to Mars by watching Matt Damon, who is stranded on the planet in the recently released movie, "The Martian." He is alone there without anyone else to play chess.

Notwithstanding the prospect of interplanetary travel, chess players at Leisure World continue meeting challenges here, as seen in the game pictured on this page. In this game, it is White's turn to move. White can win the game in two moves. Can you see it?

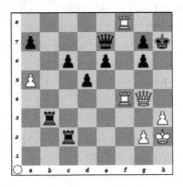

The solution to Puzzle #28 appears on page 250.

So, do not wait for summertime on Mars! Do not wait for the ice to melt! Do not wait for interplanetary travel! Play chess now!

Chess and Daylight Saving Time (DST)

November 6, 2015

By now you probably have made all the adjustments from daylight saving time (DST) to standard time on your watches, alarm clocks, wall clocks, automobiles, and kitchen appliances. Your computers, cell phones and other mobile devices may have changed automatically. You may also have used the occasion as a reminder to change the batteries in your smoke detectors. You perform this ritual twice a year: spring forward, fall back. Just because this act seems generally accepted as a way of life, doesn't mean it is without controversy.

First of all, the world cannot agree on daylight saving time (DST). Some countries do not observe it at all (India, China, Japan, South Korea, Bangladesh, and Tunisia). Countries in or near the tropics and the Equator have no need for DST because they have ample sunlight all year round. On the other hand, at least one country (Russia) has adopted DST permanently for year-round use (as of February 2011). The other 70 countries that do observe DST have varying times of implementation.

In the Northern Hemisphere, DST generally begins in March or April and ends in October, but the dates and times of day vary. For example, most of the United States begins DST on the second Sunday in March and reverts to standard time on the first Sunday in November. The change takes place when the clock reaches 2 a.m. in each time zone. In the European Union, DST (known as "Summer Time") begins on the last Sunday in March and ends on the last Sunday in October. The change takes place at 1:00 a.m. Universal Time (Greenwich Mean Time) in all EU time zones at the same moment. In the Southern Hemisphere, where everything is upside-down, DST generally starts in October and ends in March or April. In Brazil, though, since 2008, DST extends only to the third Sunday in February.

Advocates of DST proclaim, of course, that its purpose is to save energy and make better use of daylight. When clocks are set ahead one hour, sunrise and sunset will be one hour later than the day before, saving daylight for the late afternoon.

Opponents of DST contend, however, that any savings are minimal. DST, they claim, does not save time, but merely shifts the hours. Furthermore, opponents charge that DST contributes to crime, traffic and pedestrian accidents, and sleep deprivation of humans. Chickens, cows and pigs do not understand DST and keep waking up as they usually do. It is simply a nuisance to change all our clocks twice a year.

Originally countries adopted DST because of war or crises to conserve energy supplies. In the United States, in March 1918, DST was signed into law during World War I. The law was repealed seven months later, but was continued in use by some cities, including Pittsburgh, Boston, and New York, until it was reinstated in 1942 for year-round use to support the war effort.

During periods in which states and localities were free to choose when and if they would observe DST, such as in 1945-1966, great confusion arose for transportation and communication industries. To end the confusion, Congress established the Uniform Time Act of 1966, but states still were allowed exemptions from DST (e.g. Arizona) by passing a local ordinance. Congress changed the starting and ending dates of DST on several occasions: in 1974 and 1975 (following the 1973 oil embargo), in 1987 and again in 2005. In 2007, DST was extended to the first Sunday in November, presumably to provide trick-or-treaters more light and therefore more safety from traffic accidents on Halloween.

Ben Franklin, inventor, first Postmaster General, and avid chess player, sometimes is credited with originating the idea of DST. In 1784, while stationed in Paris as first U.S. envoy to France, Franklin wrote an essay (in English) to the Journal of Paris, presumably in jest, suggesting that Parisians could economize candle usage by waking up earlier than noon and making more use of natural morning light. He suggested using church bells and cannons as wake-up calls.

At Leisure World, the time system in operation has no effect on chess. Games continue regardless of the time system, as illustrated by the diagram on this page. In this game, Black is threatening checkmate by either Rook (a1 and h1). It is White's turn to move. Can White avoid checkmate? What is White's best move?

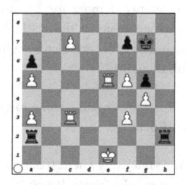

The solution to Puzzle #29 appears on page 251.

So, do not wait for Daylight Saving Time to return. Do not wait for another energy crisis. Do not wait for church bells or cannons to wake you up. Play chess now!

Time Does Not Wait for Chess

December 4, 2015

Yogi Berra may be remembered more for his unwittingly humorous statements than for his achievements on the baseball field. Although some of his remarks sound absurd or self-contradictory at first, they often convey simple, but meaningful, thoughts.

When asked what time it is, he once said, "You mean right now?" He might otherwise have asked, "Where?"

The time of day is not the same everywhere. Continental United States, for example, has four time zones; European Russia has nine; Antarctica has at least ten unofficial zones; China (which had five zones prior to 1949) now has only one time zone for the entire country (an effort to unify the country).

When we are eating lunch in Maryland at noon, the Japanese are fast asleep in Tokyo at 1 a.m. The east coast of the United States is separated from Tokyo by thirteen time zones.

Time flows constantly and endlessly, but man has found ways of manipulating it. Under Universal Coordinated Time (UTC), the globe is split into 24 time zones, one for each hour of the day. In practice, UTC is used interchangeably with GMT (Greenwich Mean Time), although their definitions differ somewhat.

Time zones would not be possible without longitude, which was created (along with latitude) by a Greek astronomer named Hipparcus about 300 years before Christ. Before that time people easily got lost. Many stood outdoors, wondering where they were and what time it was.

The longitude and latitude grid system led to other developments, which enabled sailing vessels to determine their location before the invention of global positioning systems (GPS). These gridlines are invisible, except on maps.

Time zones stretch across the Earth from east to west with the prime meridian located at Greenwich in London at the center. (In earlier days, the starting point for longitude had varied from Egypt, Greece, Spain, France, and other places, depending on which country was preeminent in celestial study at the time. For latitude, without controversy, the equator was always recognized as the center.)

A day begins at the International Date Line (IDL), an imaginary line of longitude on the Earth's surface located at about 180 degrees east (or west) of the Greenwich Meridian, halfway around the Earth. Those who cross the line going west gain a day (jump into tomorrow). Those who cross from the opposite direction lose a day (back to yesterday). Confusing as it may be, the day has to start and end somewhere.

The time zones are spaced 15 degrees of longitude apart because the Earth completes a rotation every 24 hours and there are 360 degrees of longitude. Thus, each hour the Earth rotates $1/24^{th}$ of a circle or 15 degrees.

The system is not without kinks. For example, if you stand where the borders of Norway, Finland and Russia meet, you will be in three different zones at the same time.

Before mechanical clocks were invented, sundials and hour glasses were used to indicate the passage of time and the time of day. It was not easy arriving at a worldwide standardized system for keeping time.

In the 1880s, with the growth of railroads and oceangoing vessels, the need for standardized time schedules became increasingly urgent. The situation in the United States was nearly chaotic. Some 300 different times existed across the country. All time was local.

It was not until 1884 at the International Meridian Conference in Washington, D.C. that countries reached agreement on Greenwich as the prime meridian to standardize world timekeeping and mapmaking.

Time can be important in chess. Although championship matches are usually played with time clocks, Leisure World chess games are rarely played with clocks. Thus, games are more relaxed and casual, as in the game pictured on this page. In this game, it is White's turn to move. What is White's best move?

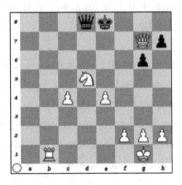

The solution to Puzzle #30 appears on page 251.

So, do not wait for the return of sundials and hourglasses! Do not wait to cross the International Date Line! Do not wait for time to stand still! Play chess now!

Climate Change and Chess

December 18, 2015

The Earth's climate has been changing for thousands of years, although no eye-witnesses have yet been found. The process is automatic, subject to the laws of astrophysics and other sciences. Many governments have decided that the process has accelerated in recent years and that it needs better regulation. Mankind is the culprit, having built cities, highways to connect the cities, automobiles, trucks, airplanes and ocean-going vessels to move people and products from place to place.

All of this requires energy, which releases carbon dioxide into the atmosphere as waste and pollution. This causes the Earth's temperature to heat up so that polar icecaps and glaciers melt faster and seas rise, flooding coastal cities and island resorts. Millions of people are likely to become refugees. Something needs to be done.

Recently, this fear motivated some 150 heads of state (along with 40,000 delegates from 195 countries) to meet in Paris from Nov.30-Dec 11 for a conference on climate change, aptly named "Conference of the Parties to the 1992 United Nations Framework Convention on Climate Change (UNFCCC)" or "COP21" for short. It is the UN's 21st conference on climate change.

The conference was budgeted to cost €170million (roughly $178 million). According to the French government, 20 percent of the cost will be borne by large firms, mostly French, such as Air France. No estimate has been made of the pollution created by the travel and transportation of all these delegates from their national capitals to Paris and back. Nevertheless, the participants were prone to hail COP21 as a big step forward.

Apparently, there is general agreement that nations should undertake commitments to limit the Earth's temperature growth to 2 degrees Celsius (3.6 degrees Fahrenheit) by 2050.

It is well known that the Earth's temperature is quite different in Alaska than in Florida. Presumably, scientists choose a place that represents the Earth's average or use other incomprehensible methods to take the planet's temperature. Whatever it is, they've been doing it for a long time.

Of all the previous UN conferences, the most ambitious took place in Kyoto in 1997 after years of preparation. It was the UN's first major initiative to combat greenhouse gas emissions and resulted in the Kyoto Protocol, which took effect on Feb. 16, 2005. To meet the Protocol's goal of reducing greenhouse gas emissions, countries undertook commitments to set targets for the period 2008-2012. Based on carbon-dioxide emission outputs in 1990, the average target was to cut emissions by 5 percent.

However, major gas-emission countries did not participate in this endeavor. At that time 37 countries and the European Union had binding goals, but China and India, which accounted for 23 and 5 percent of emissions, respectively, were exempt from reduction under the Protocol because they were listed as developing countries. The United States, accounting for nearly 15 percent of emissions, signed, but did not ratify the agreement. China and India also did not ratify the agreement. Canada signed the Protocol in 2002, but withdrew from it, effective December 2012. Twenty-one countries met their emission targets, but many of these were small countries and small polluters.

Some delegates claimed that it was unfair to expect developing countries to undertake emission restrictions which would stunt their economic growth, when pollution by the industrialized countries created the problem in the first place. Thus, as expressed by the United Nations: "the Protocol places a heavier burden on developed nations under the principle of 'common but differentiated responsibilities.'" (Huh?)

One of the most outspoken advocates for government action worldwide is former Vice President Al Gore, whose documentary, "An Inconvenient Truth," was released in 2006, heightening global awareness of the threat of climate change. Is it possible that Earth's atmosphere will obey the laws of governments rather than the laws of nature?

Chess has little to fear from emission restrictions because it is a non-polluting activity. In the diagram shown on this page, Black's only hope is for a stalemate. It is White's turn to move. What is White's best move?

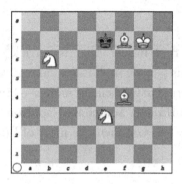

The solution to Puzzle #31 appears on Page 251.

So, do not wait for the Earth's temperature to decline. Do not wait for sea level to recede. Do not wait for more climate conferences. Play chess now!

Napoleon Plays Chess

January 22, 2016

What is Napoleon's first name? That is a trick question. Of course, Napoleon's first name is Napoleon. His last name is Bonaparte. Ordinarily, historic figures are referred to by their last names--- Hitler, Stalin, Churchill, de Gaulle, Obama, Putin, etc. Somehow Napoleon is different. He made quite a splash in history as conqueror of most of Europe and Emperor of France.

The French seem to have mixed emotions about Napoleon. They certainly do not treat him as a hero. There is no national holiday to honor him. His likeness does not appear on national currency or postage stamps. No grand boulevard or large square is named after him--- only one narrow street, Rue Bonaparte. Only two statues commemorate Napoleon in Paris: one beneath the clock tower at Les Invalides (a military hospital), the other atop a column in Place Vendôme.

Aside from his conquests, he is known for creating the foundation for much of France's legal and social system. For instance, The Napoleonic Code (established in 1804) forbade privileges based on birth, allowed freedom of religion, and specified that government jobs should go to the most qualified. The metric system was also promoted and spread by Napoleon. In 1806, Napoleon emancipated Jews (as well as Protestants in Catholic countries and Catholics in Protestant countries) from laws restricting them to ghettos, expanding their rights to property, worship, and careers. Those who view Napoleon in a favorable light would argue that he put an end to a period of lawlessness and chaos in France.

Critics, however, insist that his ultimate legacy was bankruptcy and territorial losses for France. France was weakened significantly with respect to its rivals, particularly England. Also, Napoleon had restored slavery in France's overseas colonies. His wars caused millions of military and civilian deaths in France and Europe.

Napoleon was not really French. Born in Corsica where the population was more Italian than French, Napoleon spoke French with a Corsican accent, which made his troops chuckle. He never mastered the French language and was a poor speller. Moreover, his original name was really Napoleone di Buonaparte (an Italian name).

Many Frenchmen resented his extravagant coronation in Notre Dame in December 1804, which cost 8.5 million francs or roughly as much as $125 million in today's money. After his disastrous invasion of Russia, Napoleon was forced to abdicate and was banished to the Mediterranean island of Elba. (Remember the famous palindrome: "Able was I ere I saw Elba" (reads the same backward and forward)?)

In March 1815, he escaped from Elba and returned to Paris, where he regained supporters and reclaimed his emperor title, Napoleon I. However, in June 1815, he was defeated at the Battle of Waterloo, ending France's domination of Europe. He abdicated for a second time and was exiled to the remote island of Saint Helena, in the southern Atlantic Ocean, where he died at age 52 on May 5, 1821. He was buried there until King Louis-Philippe decided to have his body exhumed and returned to Paris in 1840.

Last year marked the 200th anniversary of Napoleon's defeat at Waterloo, a town with current population of about 29,000, strategically located just 11 miles outside Brussels. In June 2015, over France's objections, Belgium issued 70,000 €2.50 coins, commemorating the event. The coins picture a monument in Waterloo and battle lines in 1815, but contain no image of Napoleon. Most of the coins will be sold to collectors in special plastic bags priced at €6. An EU rule allows euro zone countries to unilaterally issue coins if they are in an irregular denomination.

Napoleon was a chess enthusiast, although he was not a strong player due to lack of adequate time to devote to the game. However, a chess opening is named for him: "The Napoleon Opening."

You need not ride a horse, wear a two-cornered hat, or speak French with a Corsican accent to play chess in Leisure World. Residents play chess as individuals, regardless of national origin, race, religion or financial status, as in the diagram on this page. In this game, it is White's turn to move. White can mate in one move. Do you see it?

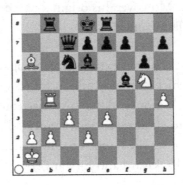

The solution to Puzzle #32 appears on page 251.

So, do not wait for a French national holiday for Napoleon! Do not wait for another defeat at Waterloo! Do not wait for French coins and stamps commemorating Napoleon! Play chess now!

Chess and February Holidays

February 5, 2016

February is a short, but significant month. Actually, February was an afterthought. It was added to the original Roman 10-month calendar (along with January) by Numa Pompilius, the second king of Rome around 700 BC. February is named after Februa, the Roman feast of purification.

In the United States, February has only one legal holiday (Presidents' Day) and one unofficial holiday (Valentine's Day). This year February is a little longer than usual because of Leap Day.

Presidents' Day used to be two days: Lincoln's Birthday (Feb. 12) and Washington's Birthday (Feb. 22). Although Lincoln's Birthday never became an official federal holiday, it was celebrated as a legal holiday in many states outside the old confederacy. Washington's Birthday, first celebrated publicly in the United States while Washington was still in office, became official in 1885, when President Chester Arthur signed a bill, making it a federal holiday.

Consolidation of the two Birthdays into a single holiday was not designed to deprive school children from a second day off. In fact, the two never were officially consolidated into Presidents' Day. It is simply that Washington's Birthday (the official holiday) was set at the third Monday of February by the Uniform Monday Holidays Act of 1968. Many Americans, however, believe the two holidays were combined to celebrate all American Presidents.

States are not obliged to adopt federal holidays. Most states have adopted Washington's Birthday, but many officially celebrate Presidents' Day. A number of the states that celebrate Washington's Birthday also recognize Lincoln's Birthday as a separate legal holiday. Maryland and seven other states officially celebrate President's Day [singular], while Texas and seven other states and Puerto Rico officially celebrate Presidents' Day [plural]. New Jersey and three other states celebrate Presidents Day [no possessive, no apostrophe]. So much for uniformity.

Although Valentine's Day (Feb 14) is not an official holiday, it is commercially significant. More greeting cards (about 150 million per year) are sold for Valentine's Day than for any other holiday, except Christmas. In recent years, Valentine's Day has generated about $18-$19 billion in retail sales, including greeting cards, candy, flowers, jewelry, and romantic dinners. The holiday is based on the ancient Roman festival of Lupercalia, a fertility celebration commemorated annually on February 15. Pope Gelasius I recast this pagan festival as a Christian feast day circa 496, declaring February 14 to be St. Valentine's Day.

Valentine's Day is celebrated in various ways in other countries. In the Philippines, it is celebrated with mass public weddings (thousands each year). In Japan, women present chocolates to men. In Ghana, the world's largest exporter of cocoa beans, it is celebrated as "Chocolate Day." Guatemala celebrates El Día del Cariño, marking the holiday with parades of revelers dressed in feathered masks and Mayan clothing. In South Africa, youths pin the name of their sweetheart to their sleeve, in a tradition that is known in the country as Lupercalia, the aforementioned ancient Roman fertility festival.

Leap Day is a day used to compensate for the failure of the calendar to end in an even number of days. It takes 365 ¼ days for the Earth to complete its orbit around the sun, not just 365 days. To account for the extra ¼ day, a leap day is added to the end of February. Why February? Because that is the way the Romans did it.

You do not need a Roman holiday (or an official federal holiday) to play chess at Leisure World. In the game pictured on this page White is threatening checkmate on the next move by capturing Black's Pawn at g7 with the Queen from e7. However, it is Black's turn to move. What is Black's best move?

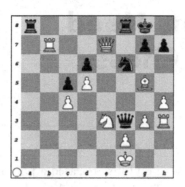

The solution of Puzzle #33 appears on page 251.

So, do not wait for uniform spelling of President's Day. Do not wait for Valentine's Day to become an official federal holiday. Do not wait for next leap year. Play chess now!

Presidents Need
Time for Chess

February 19, 2016

In August 2012, the White House released a photo of President Obama firing a shotgun at Camp David. It is not clear why the photo was released. We would have preferred to see a photo of President Obama playing chess.

The President's job, however, has become so demanding that there is little time for him to play a serious game. Perhaps Presidents Day should be set aside to give the President a chance to play a suitable opponent and provide ample photo opportunities for the press.

More recently, the Republican Presidential campaign debates have generated a great deal of information about the candidates. The public now knows where the candidates were born, what they eat for breakfast, and how they exercise. However, the public does not know how well they play chess or whether they play at all. The candidates themselves have tried to explain the knowledge, skills and attributes they have that will make them a winning candidate. None of them, however, has mentioned chess-playing as one of those skills.

It is known, however, that Bernie Sanders plays chess because his wife mentioned in a television interview that he taught his grandchildren how to play chess. Also, Donald Trump has been quoted as saying that "We all know that chess is a game of strategy. So is business." Otherwise, we know little about chess-playing by the candidates.

Chess-playing is not generally recognized as a qualification for becoming President of the United States. Yet, many of our Presidents have been avid chess players. In fact, more than half of our Presidents have been identified as chess players (24 of 44). This has not gone unnoticed by some political analysts.

For example, a University of Minnesota website of the Humphrey School of Public Affairs (umn.edu) once noted that "None of the last five Republican presidents were chess players, whereas eight of the last nine Democratic presidents played the game." The article went on to say: "Since the Chester Arthur administration in the early 1880s, 89 percent of Democratic presidents have been chess players (8 of 9), compared to just 29 percent of Republicans (4 of 14)."

Regardless of the political implications, in honor of President's Day (sometimes spelled "Presidents' Day" in the plural or "Presidents Day" with no apostrophe at all), here is a list of Presidents who played chess: George Washington, Thomas Jefferson, James Madison, James Monroe, John Quincy Adams, Andrew Jackson, Martin Van Buren, Millard Fillmore, Abraham Lincoln, Ulysses S. Grant, Rutherford Hayes, James A. Garfield, Grover Cleveland, Theodore Roosevelt, William Howard Taft, Woodrow Wilson, Calvin Coolidge, Franklin D. Roosevelt, Harry S. Truman, Dwight D. Eisenhower, John F. Kennedy, Jimmy Carter, William Jefferson Clinton (a member of the Georgetown University chess team in 1968), and Barack Obama.

Chess is not regulated by the federal government. Chess sets can be bought by anyone and can be used by anyone, regardless of race, age, gender, or political affiliation. No background check is required. Thus, chess is played regularly at Leisure World, as in the game shown in the accompanying diagram. In this game, Black is one move away from checkmating the White King (by capturing the Pawn at d5 with the Bishop at b7). However, it is White's turn to move. Can White avoid losing by checkmate? What is White's best move?

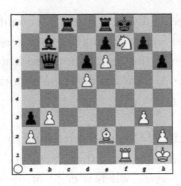

The solution to Puzzle #34 appears on page 251.

So, do not wait for Presidential candidates with chess-playing skills. Do not wait for uniform spelling of Presidents' Day. Do not wait for regulation of the sale of chess sets by the federal government. Play chess now!

Advertising Chess
on Television

March 4, 2016

Chess is not getting its fair share of television time--- not even in the commercials. It is time to modernize chess advertising.

Just imagine what could have been done when Peyton Manning's Denver Broncos won the Super Bowl. An announcer chases him on the playing field, sticks a microphone in his face, and says, "Peyton Manning, you've just won the Super Bowl. What will you do next?" Peyton smiles and says, "I'm going to play a really challenging game of chess!" It leaves the audience thinking: "That's what we should do."

Here is another example. Two climbers, weighed down by heavy gear and snow shoes, reach the top of a mountain. They are out of breath, simply exhausted. They see a door and open it. Inside is a crowded, bustling bar with a party atmosphere. People are drinking their favorite brew in bottles, watching a chess game on TV screens, and rooting for their favorite chess player, who is engaged in a tough match against a gorilla, miles away from the mountain. The gorilla has a wicked smile on his face. He is winning. Just then, however, the human makes a brilliant move. The crowd in the Chess Bar goes wild. The gorilla is noticeably embarrassed. The commercial ends with these words flashed across the screen: "Root for chess! It's worth the climb!"

In another commercial, real people (not actors) are trying to determine the automobile brand with all the luxurious features. A half dozen of these real people are gathered around the car, chattering to each other that it must be an expensive brand. They open the back door of the car and find a man and a woman in the back seat, playing chess. At the same time, they realize that the car is a popular, inexpensive brand. They all want to buy the reasonably-priced car that is equipped with a built-in chess set. "Give me the keys," says one of the real people.

In a commercial at a fast food restaurant, featuring oversized cheeseburgers, several tables are reserved for chess games. Spectators are hunched over the tables, viewing the boards, munching on their burgers, and washing them down with cola drinks. They are all having fun. The commercial ends with an announcer proclaiming, "Fast food and slow chess: it's a winning combo!!!" This advertisement will sell more chess sets (or burgers).

The opening scene of another commercial pictures a man and a woman in casual clothes. They are standing very close together, smiling lovingly and knowingly at each other. Not a word is said between them. In the final scene, they are sitting in separate bathtubs with their backs to the camera, evidently nude, but playing chess side-by-side. As the bathtubs float into the distance, an off-screen announcer issues a warning, "If the game lasts more than 4 hours, call your doctor."

It is clear that the chess industry has missed out on numerous opportunities to advertise effectively. At Leisure World, however, Chess Club members already are smitten. They need no encouragement to play chess.

In the game shown on the following page, it is White's turn to move. What is White's best move?

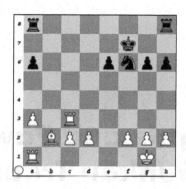

The solution to Puzzle #35 appears on page 251.

So, do not wait for better TV commercials! Do not wait for a car with a built-in chess set! Do not wait for 4 hours to call your doctor! Play chess now!

Are Knights and Pawns Among Sunken Treasures?

March 18, 2016

Archaeologists are seeking evidence that chess was played at sea hundreds of years ago. The world's seas are littered with as many as three million sunken ships, according to UNESCO estimates. Recovering cargo from sunken ships could become a lucrative international industry.

Not all are treasure ships, some of which carried gold and minerals from the colonies to finance wars in Europe. Many, however, if found, could help answer historians' questions about how ships were loaded and managed hundreds of years ago--- even whether they were equipped with chess sets.

UNESCO's Convention on the Protection of the Undersea Cultural Heritage is designed to discourage commercial exploitation of these shipwrecks (as well as to protect them from damages from the sea and from looters who steal artifacts and sell them for personal profit). The Convention took effect in 2009, having been ratified by 51 countries--- but not the United States.

Recently a treasure ship was discovered in the Caribbean off the coast of Colombia. The vessel is a Spanish galleon, named San Jose, which sank there in 1708. It may contain as much as $17 billion in precious metals and gems, including 11 million gold coins from the Spanish colonies. There are conflicting claims over who is entitled to the cargo--- the Colombian government or the salvage company. The Spanish government may also stake a claim.

Sea Search Armada (the salvage company) claims that the Colombian government recognized the potential value of recovering the wreck and purposefully changed the existing law to cut out the research team which found the wreck 700 feet below the surface in 1982.

The Colombian government has denied the company's claim and is already planning to build a museum dedicated to the San Jose in Cartagena, hoping to draw more tourists into the site of the wreck.

In another recent discovery, an ancient Roman vessel was found off the coast of Italy, loaded with 3,000 jars of fish sauce--- or garum. The find was announced by archaeologists last December, following a two-year search. The ship dates back to the first or second century AD.

Italy's Ministry of Cultural Heritage started a project in 2004 to register all underwater archaeological sites along its long coastlines. In Italy, tourists can do their own exploration by snorkeling and scuba diving in an underwater archaeological park at the west end of the gulf of Naples.

It is known that chess has been played at sea, but proof may be lacking. Some say a chess game was in progress in the card room of the Titanic when the ship hit an iceberg in the Atlantic. The chess players were so absorbed in their games that they failed to notice that the ship was sinking. They were oblivious to the band playing "Nearer My God to Thee," and continued their games during the entire tragic incident.

It is also known that the cruise ship that lost power and propulsion in the Gulf of Mexico several years ago was not equipped with enough chess sets to meet passenger needs. Imagine drifting aimlessly at sea for several days without electricity and without a decent chess game to occupy the time.

The cruise line should have announced that, for future sailings, each cabin would be equipped with regulation size chess boards and pieces, stowed alongside life jackets. Chess boards would be inflatable to enable flotation and pieces would plug into holes in the board. During the mandatory life boat drill, all passengers would be informed of the location of chess sets. A small flashlight and whistle also would be stowed nearby to attract other players in case of emergency.

It is always safe to play chess in Clubhouse II at Leisure World. No special equipment is needed. Witness the game pictured on this page. It is early in the game, but White has a commanding lead and it is White's turn to move. What is White's best move?

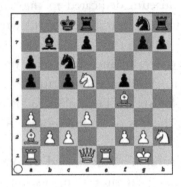

The solution to Puzzle #36 apears on page 252.

So, do not wait for a floating chess set! Do not wait for sunken treasures! Do not wait for registration as an undersea cultural heritage site! Play chess now!

Chess and the Media

April 1, 2016

Chess was never a big hit on the radio. Sound effects never quite simulated the atmosphere of a chess game and radio announcers never could quite fill in the gaps between moves with colorful anecdotes. The audience is silent and there are no cheerleaders or mascots. Crowd noise and cheering are discouraged, kept to a minimum, or totally absent.

Radio stations are missing out. The gaps between chess moves are conducive to analyses and commercials. Unlike hockey games, they provide lots of time for advertising. Also, championship games can be highlighted on all-news broadcasts with updates every ten minutes or with breaking news flashes when a move is made.

Visualize the announcer reporting on the last move. "Black has just moved the Pawn to the f5 square, threatening White's Queen. White's Queen is protecting two other squares. White has only five minutes left on his clock. Will White move the Queen or counter-attack? Will time run out? We'll let you know as soon as it happens. Keep your radio tuned to this station!"

However, radio executives did not see it that way. Perhaps, the advertising sponsors did not believe that chess players would constitute a profitable market. They never buy anything. They are too busy playing chess and have no spare time.

In the heyday of radio--- back in the forties and fifties--- Comedian Fred Allen described the job of an NBC radio executive as follows. Each morning the executive comes to work and finds a molehill on his desk. His task is to build it into a mountain before the end of the day.

Gaps of silence on radio could also be filled with music, but chess was never popular in the music world either. Probably the only song about chess was the title song of the stage play "Chess," a musical which opened in London in 1986, where it played for three years. It opened on Broadway in 1988, but survived only for two months.

So chess never made it on radio and never made it on Broadway.

Chess was better in motion pictures. Recall the 1968 version of "The Thomas Crown Affair." Steve McQueen, elegantly dressed in suit and tie and smoking a fine cigar, is sitting in a well furnished, but dimly lit drawing room with Faye Dunaway, dressed in a sensuous, backless black evening gown and gently sipping from a wine glass. They are playing chess, of course. No one else is in the room. A small fire is crackling in the fireplace. Soft music is playing in the background. They move chess pieces slowly and look at each other sexily between moves. They touch knees, then fingers. Within seven minutes, they are in the sack.

Now, nothing like this is going to happen at Clubhouse II in Leisure World. However, you might end up in a game like the one pictured on the following page. Black has just moved the Queen to d5, threatening White's Rook at b7. It is White's move. Can White save the Rook? Can he win the game? What is White's best move?

The solution to Puzzle #37 appears on page 252.

So, do not wait for a chess broadcast on radio! Do not wait for a scene from The Thomas Crown Affair! Do not wait for a breaking news flash! Play chess now!

Feeling Lucky? Chess by the Numbers

April 15, 2016

None of us is superstitious. (Knock on wood.) However, some of us believe that numbers can be lucky or unlucky and some of us take it very seriously. For example, in China, where the number 4 is considered unlucky--- simply because the Chinese word for 4 sounds like the word for (gulp) "death" --- many buildings in Beijing and other cities are missing the fourth floor. The floor numbers skip "4," just as buildings in the USA skip the 13th. Floor numbers in taller buildings in China may skip from 39 to 50 to avoid all those 4s. No need to tempt fate.

Think of the implications for American sports:

- baseball without a fourth inning;
- football without a 40-yard line;
- football and basketball without a fourth quarter; and
- college basketball without a Final Four.

In music, Beethoven's Symphony #4 and others would have to be renumbered, as well as piano, violin and horn concertos. Quartets would be outlawed.

And when would we celebrate Independence Day, if not on July 4th?

On the other hand, the number 8 in China is lucky --- because the word for 8 sounds like the Chinese word for "fortune" or "wealth." This could have enormous influence on businesses. Hotels, for example, may place an 8 in front of each room number. So if you are on the fifth floor, your room number may be 8501 (instead of merely 501). Of course, the hotel may charge more for room numbers that contain an 8 (and guests may be willing to pay more).

People will actually pay large sums of money to get phone numbers and auto license plates with 8s. In August 2003, a Chinese airline bought the phone number "88888888" for about $300,000. Flight numbers throughout Asia often have multiple eights. A man in Hangzhou offered to sell his license plate reading A88888 for ¥1.12 million (roughly $164,000).

Moreover, in 2008, the Beijing Summer Olympic Committee set the opening of the games on 08/08/08 at eight minutes and eight seconds after 8:00 pm! This is especially lucky because of the repetition. Double anything is particularly auspicious. A Chinese man in Las Vegas purchased bulb #8 and #88 from the Welcome to Fabulous Las Vegas sign on August 8, 2008.

Eight is also considered a lucky number in Japan. It is thought of as a holy number as in ancient times.

Coincidentally, a chessboard has eight squares across and eight squares vertically. So, it must be lucky to play chess. Chess players at Leisure World, however, do not necessarily play chess for luck. They are mostly absorbed in the game and could care less about anything else. In the game pictured on the following page, for instance, White is outmanned and the Queen is under attack by the Black Bishop. The outlook is bleak. What is White's best move?

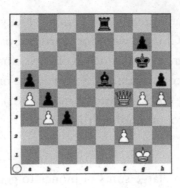

The solution to Puzzle #38 appears on page 252.

So, do not wait for a room on the eighth floor! Do not wait for a phone number with multiple eights! Do not wait for a license plate with eight eights! Play chess now!

Phobias and Chess

May 20, 2016

Those who suffer from paraskevidekatriaphobia (fear of Friday the 13th) will take comfort in knowing that Friday the 13th occurs only once this year. It is in the month of May. Once they get by this month, they should have no fears until 2017, when it will occur twice (in January and October).

Many who have never suffered from this fear may be totally unsympathetic to those who have. It is not great fun. Symptoms vary from person to person and range from nervousness to anxiety to hysteria to outright panic.

Hypochondriacs are advised not to read the following list of symptoms:

- Hyperventilation
- Rapid heart rate
- Nervous giggling
- Lightheadedness or dizziness
- Refusing to leave home until the end of the day
- Crying, screaming, trying to flee

Sufferers of this phobia may also indulge in ritualistic behavior. Some may hang shoes outside the window to repel evil. Some may eat garlic that day or wear an asafoetida bag around the neck. Some may walk around the room 13 times each hour. Some may even refuse to play chess on that day.

Oh yes, in case you are wondering about it, an asafoetida bag is like a tea bag containing asafoetida--- leaves or powder from a potent, foul smelling plant that will keep the devil away. It will also keep all your friends away. It is, however, fun to pronounce (asa-fetida) and is regarded fondly sometimes as "the world's most repulsive spice."

In two recent years, Friday the 13th has occurred only once during the year (2010, 2011). It occurred three times in 2012 and 2015. Despite these variances, it is entirely predictable that the dreaded day will occur twice in each of the years from 2017 to 2020. Check it out.

The more one knows about Friday the 13th, the less fear that bad things will happen on that day. Bad things can happen any day. And usually do.

There is a related phobia: triskaidekaphobia (fear of the number 13). People with this phobia have more to fear because the 13th occurs every month regardless of the weather, holidays, or scheduled public events. Oscar Levant, the entertaining pianist of the 30's and 40's, was known to fear the number 13 and practically made it famous all by himself.

As a matter of fact, phobias are fairly common. Just think of all the people who are afraid of flying; those who are afraid of crowds and confined spaces; darkness, thunder, and lightning; snakes, spiders, birds, sharks, and germs.

If you feel you must have a phobia (and you do not yet have one), there are a large number of phobias from which to choose, many of which you may never have heard of, such as: eisoptrophobia, ataxaphobia, bacteriaphobia, achluophobia, nychtophobia, scotophobia, ichthyophobia, papyrophobia, lepidopterophobia, mottephobia, and botanophobia. (We sell more dictionaries this way.)

Avid chess players at Leisure World are not concerned about Friday the 13th. Many are not even aware of the calendar, especially those who suffer from hyperchessmania, a state of mind in which the individual continually seeks to play more chess without respect to the time of day.

In the game pictured on this page, White moved the Pawn to b7, seeking to promote it to a Queen on the next move. Black then captured White's Knight at g5. Did Black have a better move?

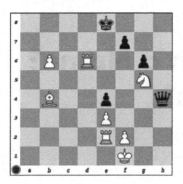

The solution to Puzzle #39 appears on Page 252.

So, do not wait to for an asafoetida bag! Do not wait for a world free of phobias! Above all, do not wait for a year in which Friday the 13th does not occur! Play chess now!

What's In a Name?
Redskins?

June 3, 2016

Although it is not even football season, one of the hottest topics of discussion in Washington these days (aside from the Presidential campaign and dysfunctional government) is the name of the city's professional football team.

Registration of the team name and logo was cancelled by the U.S. Patent and Trademark Office (USPTO) in 2014, a matter which currently is under appeal in the U.S. Court of Appeals for the Fourth Circuit in Richmond, Virginia. USPTO took the action because Federal trademark law does not permit registration of trademarks that "may disparage" individuals or groups. The "Redskin" name is regarded as a racial slur and is offensive to many Native American Indians.

In the most recent development, though, 90 percent of Native American Indians in a Washington Post poll indicated that they did not find the Redskin name offensive. Groups representing Native Americans, however, reject the results of the poll. So we will just have to wait and see whether this poll makes any difference in the case.

In recent years, President Obama and Members of Congress have weighed in to get a name change. The Senate Majority Leader declared that he will not attend another Washington home game until the team changes its name. Fifty Senators signed a letter to the NFL Commissioner, requesting a name change. A bill seeking a name change was introduced in the House and is pending. In addition, a federal judge has ordered that no court documents should refer to the team by name, but only as the Washington Team.

Long-time Redskin fans are attached to the name and regard it as a symbol of pride. They resist a name change for fear that the team's traditions will be lost.

To paraphrase William Shakespeare: "What's in a name? That which we call a [Redskin] by any other name would smell [of sweat]." There are many alternatives for re-naming the Redskins, including Warriors, Pigskins, Hogs, and others which would be less offensive to various groups.

A suitable name might be The Red Kings since it has the same sound as Redskins. The same burgundy and gold colors could be used for uniforms and commercials. The same fight song could be used ("Hail to the Red Kings...."). The team's logo could be the King of Hearts and the King of Diamonds. These are only playing cards, inanimate objects (which sometimes resemble how the team plays). The only group that might be offended by the name would be the Monarchists, but only the red ones.

One professional basketball team, the Sacramento Kings, has a similar name. Oddly enough, the name has received complaints from anti-Monarchists, who believe that the name unjustly glorifies totalitarian rulers. Hmmmm?

A name change might open new money-making opportunities for the team, such as a new line of Red Kings branded merchandise or the sale of naming rights. Naming the stadium "Fedex Field" already brings in millions of dollars each year. While a deal is being negotiated, player uniforms could read: "YOUR NAME HERE" across the chest.

In any event, unlike football, chess is not affected by team names and logos. At tournaments, teams may be named after their locations (the "US team" or the "New Jersey team," etc.), although contestants generally play under their own names. At Leisure World, with monarchies at both ends of the board, the Royal Game is played by individuals, who play for their own pleasure and not for team glory, as in the game pictured on this page.

In this game, White is winning and threatening a checkmate at b7. White has just moved the Pawn at a5 to a6, putting more pressure on Black's King. Black cannot capture White's Pawn at a6 because the Pawn at b7 is pinned by White's Bishop at f3. Black's Queen at d7 is protecting the Pawn at b7. It is Black's turn to move. What is Black's best move?

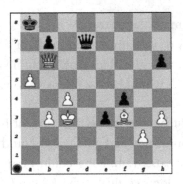

The solution to Puzzle #40 appears on page 252.

So, do not wait for football season. Do not wait for Congress to act. Do not wait for a politically correct name. Play chess now!

24-Year-Old Champ Humbles LW Chess Club

June 3, 2016

On Friday, May 20, Scott Low, a National Master since the age of 16, played six Leisure World chess players simultaneously--- and beat them all. To become a National Master, a player must obtain a rating of over 2200 from the U.S. Chess Federation. Only 1% of all chess players become Masters. Approximately 5% become Experts (rating between 2000 and 2199).

In simultaneous play, Scott allowed LW players to play White or Black. LW players were seated at tables (in Room 2 of Clubhouse II), while Scott walked around from board to board and made his moves in seconds. He also played one game blindfolded and won the game handily. Quite impressive!

Currently 24 years old, Scott is a graduate of John F. Kennedy High School in Silver Spring. He won two chess tuition scholarships to UMBC and University of Texas at Dallas, but decided to go to University of Maryland (College Park) for the Aerospace Engineering program. He is currently employed by a contractor associated with NASA.

Scott has won five Maryland State Scholastic Championships and tied for first in two National High School Championships. His biggest money prize was at the World Open in Philadelphia in 2009 when he tied for first in the expert section, winning $10,500.

Present at the exhibition were Scott's father, Tim, and his grandfather, Jim --- three generations of Lows. The LW Chess Club has scheduled another Simultaneous Chess event with another Champ on Monday, June 6.

Chess Gets a Colonoscopy

June 17, 2016

Colonoscopies are not great fun, particularly the dietary requirements in the days immediately prior to the procedure. Eat no solids the day before and drink an overly salty liquid solution (or take special pills) and drink lots of water. The preparation can be worse than the procedure itself.

But the procedure need not be all that grim. On the day of the procedure, after you dress up in that classy light blue paper gown which ties in the back, get your doctor to tell you a joke before he does the job. Yes. Doctors are specially trained to tell jokes as a means of calming the patient.

When you ask for a joke, you will be pleasantly surprised at your doctor's reaction. Doctors have an ample supply of jokes, all very professional, of course.

He may tell you the one about the patient who suspects that his wife's hearing is failing. So he asks the doctor how he can tell if his wife is losing her hearing. The doctor thinks for a moment and then says, "When your wife is sitting in the living room with her back to you, get fifteen feet behind her and say, "Honey, what time is dinner?" If she doesn't answer, get a little closer and say, "Honey, what time is dinner?" If she still doesn't answer, get right behind her chair and say, "Honey, what time is dinner?" See how she reacts.

The patient thinks this is a good idea. When he gets home, he tries it out. His wife is sitting in the living room reading a book. He stands about fifteen feet away and says, "Honey, what time is dinner?" No answer. He moves closer and says, "Honey, what time is dinner? No answer. He moves directly behind her chair and says, "Honey, what time is dinner?" She turns around and says: "For the THIRD time, it's 5 o'clock."

If you think this is funny, you can laugh, but if you've heard this joke before, tell your doctor and do not hesitate to ask for another joke. He may tell you the one about the 85-year-old patient. Dugan, a gentleman of that age, visits his doctor for a checkup and receives good news. He is as healthy as a 40-year-old. He is elated. He is euphoric. He thanks the doctor. On his way out, he tells the receptionist: "Wow, the doctor thinks I have the body of a 40-year-old. I feel great!" He is at the exit when he sees a good looking lady sitting near the door, reading a magazine. He stops and says to her, "Excuse me. How old do you think I am?"

She looks at him. She says, "Come closer." He moves closer. "No, I mean closer than that." He moves up to her. She zips open his fly, reaches inside, and moves her hand around. After 30 seconds she says, "You're 85 years old."

Dugan thinks this is amazing. "I think that's amazing," he says. "How did you figure out I was 85 years old?" She is unflappable. She says, "I heard you tell the receptionist." (Bavababoom! Drumroll! Cymbals! Laughter!)

So when your procedure is complete, you will sleep a bit and wake up refreshed. You will feel hungry and you will remember the joke. Even colonoscopies can be enjoyable, at least if the doctor tells the joke right.

LW chess players are not great fans of colonoscopies, especially if they interfere with their chess schedules. Chess games, of course, are not permitted during medical procedures. You will never see a colonoscopy in Clubhouse II, where the LW Chess Club plays. Afterward, however, chess may be played, as in the game pictured on the following page.

In this game, White has just moved his Pawn to d7, where it can be promoted to a Queen on the next move. In that case, Black will have to lose his Rook when it captures the Queen at d8. Black will then lose his Rook to the White Rook now located at d3. Black would then be severely handicapped. It is Black's turn to move. What is Black's best move?

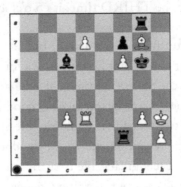

The solution to Puzzle #41 appears on page 252.

So, do not wait for your next colonoscopy! Do not wait for a doctor to tell you a joke! Do not wait for a good looking lady to tell you your age! Play chess now!

National Mammal Played Part in American Heritage

July 1, 2016

The United States now has something it never had before: a National Mammal. It is about time. The United States has had a National Bird (the eagle), a National Tree (the oak) and a National Flower (the rose), but when President Obama signed the National Bison Legacy Act in May, bison lovers finally could take pride in having a national symbol of their own.

There was no competition for the designation, although white-tailed deer are the mammal symbol of eleven states (AR, GA, IL, MI, MS, NE, NH, OH, PA, and SC), while bison are the State Mammal of only three (KS, OK, and WY). It was purely a matter of politics, led by ranchers, Indian tribes and conservationists, who aimed to raise awareness of the bison's historic importance.

Bison are also known as buffalo, although there is a slight physical difference between them. The bison themselves do not know the difference as many bison have been interbred with buffalo.

Bison helped shape the lifestyle of Native Americans in the Great Plains and are an important part of American heritage. Native Americans lived alongside herds of these migratory animals for many years, using their meat for food, their hides for shelter; in fact, using every part of the animal, including their horns and hair.

Tens of millions of bison roamed the continental U.S. prior to the arrival of settlers from European countries. Estimates of the original population of prairie bison range upward to 200 million (PBS TV 1998).

Bison are enormous animals, often more than a dozen feet long and six feet tall, weighing as much as 2,000 pounds. So they are difficult to hug. They are also difficult to catch because they can run as fast as 35 miles an hour despite their weight. Usually, however, they spend much of their time eating grass, resting, and chewing their cud. They are said to have poor eyesight and hearing (often bumping into each other in a crowded herd), but their sense of smell is excellent (although they themselves don't smell so good).

The number of bison began to decline drastically as European settlers moved westward in America. The introduction of horses and guns into the region made it easier to kill bison. Traders and trappers moved in, making their living by selling meat and hides. By the 1870s, hundreds of thousands of buffalo hides were shipped eastward each year. Construction of the Transcontinental Railroad hastened the decline of the bison population. William "Buffalo Bill" Cody was hired by the Kansas Pacific Railroad to hunt the bison to feed thousands of rail laborers for years. Massive hunting parties arrived from the east to kill bison for sport from the windows of their railroad coaches.

By 1880, only a few thousand animals remained. A survey in 1905 indicated that the bison population had shrunk to 1,089. Over the years, joint action by various groups arrested the decline and the bison population began rebounding.

Today, more than 500,000 bison live in North America, including those in the 5,000 privately ranched herds. The largest rancher is Ted Turner (founder of CNN), who supplies meat for his 44 Ted's Montana Grill restaurants in 16 states. Turner Enterprises manages over 51,000 bison.

To celebrate National Bison Day on November 5 this year, you can hug a bison, grow a beard, eat a buffalo steak, or attend commemorative events.

LW chess players do not consume buffalo meat, especially during chess games. In the game pictured on this page, Black is poised to capture White's Knight, but it is White's turn to move. What is White's best move?

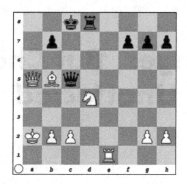

The solution to Puzzle# 42 appears on page 252.

So, do not wait for National Bison Day. Do not wait to hug a bison. Do not wait for bison to become extinct. Play chess now!

Life Changes, But Chess Remains Unaffected

July 15, 2016

Changes are always happening. We are getting accustomed to change even though its tempo keeps speeding up. Change is a way of life. This was known in ancient Greece. A Greek philosopher named Heraclitus became famous for his view that ever-present change is a fundamental essence of the universe. He is given credit for the quotation: "Nothing is permanent, except change." Or maybe it was: "The only thing that is constant is change."

That was Heraclitus, not Herodotus. They were not even contemporaries. Heraclitus was at least 50 years older than Herodotus. Both were philosophers, though. They lived at a time when life was simpler, men were known only by a single name, and the years were counted backwards. Heraclitus lived from 535-475 BCE and Herodotus lived from 484-425 BCE. Herodotus became much more famous because he was a contemporary of Socrates and is known as "The father of history."

In any event, changes take place, not only in the weather, but in government and politics, technology, and social systems. Heraclitus never suspected that Britain would vote to leave the European Union. Nor did he expect that sound recordings would start with phonographs, move to 8-tracks, to cassette tapes, to compact disks and now to streaming. Nor did he know that horses would be replaced by automobiles, that is, horseless carriages. Nor did he realize that marriages could take place between people of the same sex. He was a philosopher, not a soothsayer. Note that the word "soothsayer" is now obsolete. A soothsayer was someone who saw and told the truth, not a predictor of the future.

Changes in technology can make people and jobs obsolete. The end of horse transportation, for example, put an end to buggy whips (the quintessential symbol of obsolescence), as well as to horseshoes, hitching posts, blacksmiths and stablemen. Sales of horse manure for fertilizer also suffered. Indoor plumbing ended the manufacture of outhouses and chamber pots. Changes in personal habits put an end to snuff, spittoons, and ash trays. Changes in fashion reduced the need for powdered wigs, men's hats, knickers, and spats.

Changes in medical practices ended the procedures for cupping and lobotomies. The advent of personal computers and printers ended the need for typewriters, carbon paper, and mimeographs. Automation overtook jobs as telephone operators, service station attendants and elevator operators. Robots now install windshields and paint cars. Even the measurement of time has changed from water clocks and hour glasses to jeweled lever and battery operated watches and clocks.

Moore's law--- the epitome of technological progress --- is now in danger of extinction. This law, introduced in 1965 by electrical engineer George Moore (who became co-founder of Intel Corporation), theorized that, through technological advancements, computer power would double every year (changed in 1975 to every two years). Thus, certain computer processors or parts would become obsolete every two years. Now there is concern that it will take longer than that to produce the next generation of microprocessors. The physical space for additional transistors is running out. Moore's Law itself, therefore, may become obsolete.

Chess is relatively unaffected by change. Few, if any, rules have changed since 1560 in Spain, when pawns were allowed to move two spaces instead of one on their first move. This helped to speed up the game openings. At the Leisure World Chess Club, it is the endings that need to be speeded up, as in the game pictured on the following page. In this game, the players have just exchanged Rooks at f3. White's Queen is now threatened by Black's Rook, which is protected by the Bishop at d5. It is White's turn to move. What is White's best move?

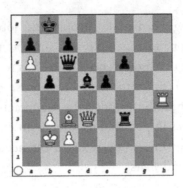

The solution to Puzzle #43 appears on page 252.

So do not wait for next year's fashions. Do not wait for the return of spittoons. Do not wait for more computer power. Play chess now!

A Good Year for Elephants--- and Chess

August 5, 2016

World Elephant Day will be celebrated on August 12 by people in various cities and by elephants themselves. Elephants will parade and frolic, eat a vegetarian lunch, and march to a river, where they will spray each other with cool water. People will celebrate by buying elephant coloring books and T-shirts with slogans ("Save the Elephants," "I Love Elephants"). People will also visit zoos and listen to speeches.

This has been a good year for elephants. In recent months, the United States and China, major consumer countries, both took action to ban illegal trade in ivory, which comes from the tusks of elephants. At least seven other countries have taken similar actions.

- In April, Kenya's President set fire to 105 tons of ivory in Nairobi National Park, the largest stockpile ever burned (equivalent to the tusks of about 8,000 elephants, said to be worth some $150 million on the black market).
- In May, China destroyed 1,500 pounds of seized ivory tusks and carvings in Beijing. (An elephant stomp would have been appropriate.)
- In June, more than a ton of ivory and ivory products were pulverized by a 50,000 pound rock crusher at a ceremony in Times Square. (No word on what happened to the fragments.) The event

was well attended, but the crowd was not nearly as large as for a New Year's Eve celebration.
- All the various events worldwide illustrate the determination of nations to end poaching and save the elephants.

Tens of thousands of African elephants are killed by poachers each year, which could lead to their extinction in the near future. Centuries ago an estimated 26 million elephants roamed the African continent. By the early 1900s, the number had declined to about 10 million. Currently the population of African elephants is little more than 400,000. Similar problems plague Asian elephants, whose population has shrunk from an estimated 200,000 at the turn of the century, to no more than 35-40,000 today.

Many of the countries where elephants live (37 countries in Africa; 12 in Asia) are poor countries, which earn revenue from the sale of hunting licenses. One report indicates that it may be cheaper to buy a live elephant than to buy a hunting license ($300,000 for an elephant, $400,000 for a license).

Zimbabwe wants to use revenue from hunting licenses to finance conservation programs for elephants. It is a practice favored by the International Union for Conservation of Nature (IUCN). Kill some to save others. IUCN originally sponsored the Convention on International Trade in Endangered Species (CITES), the body which regulates international trade in ivory.

As the price of ivory soared (to as much as $2,100 per kilo), poachers became more organized, using automatic weapons, motorized vehicles, and airplanes to chase and kill thousands of elephants. Recent government actions, however, should discourage these activities (prices already have been cut in half).

So, this year elephants can rightfully celebrate during this sixth annual World Elephant Day!

In Leisure World, the Chess Club can take pride that none of its games are played with ivory chess sets. In the game pictured on this page, Black's King is in check by the White Knight at d7. If Black moves the King to get out of check, the White Knight can capture Black's Queen at f6. But Black can capture the White Knight with the Knight at b6. What is Black's best move?

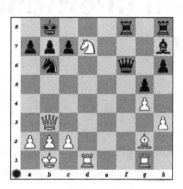

The solution to Puzzle #44 appears on page 253.

So do not wait for an outright end to poaching. Do not wait for a hunting license. Do not wait for next World Elephant Day. Play chess now!

Chess Is an International Language

August 19, 2016

The world has about 7,000 languages. (No wonder we cannot understand each other.) Of those languages, roughly 90 percent are spoken by fewer than 100,000 people.

More people speak Mandarin Chinese than any other language. As the second leading language, there is controversy over whether Spanish is spoken by more people than English. Estimates vary. Clearly, though, English is the most widely spoken and most taught language in the world. Thanks to British colonization and, more recently, computer and internet technology, English has become the second language in many countries and is the most universal.

At one time Latin was seen as an international language, but currently it is regarded as a "dead" language. Hundreds of languages have become extinct in recent years. About 2,500 more are at risk of extinction, according to UNESCO (the United Nations Education, Scientific and Cultural Organization).

On the other hand, the ancient language of Hebrew has been revived and is now spoken by five million people in Israel and nine million worldwide. It is one of two official languages in Israel; Arabic is the other. Hebrew is read backwards (but it is not spoken backwards).

The African continent, with 53 countries, has about 2,000 languages. India has about 780 languages.

The European Union has 24 official languages, now that Croatia has become a member country (while you were not watching). All European laws must be translated into each of the official languages. The EU employs 1,750 linguists plus 600 support staff--- probably the largest translation service in the world--- at an annual cost of some $1.5 billion. (Who said we do not know how to create jobs?) If Britain leaves the EU, English may no longer be an official language of the EU, but could simply become a "working" language.

Esperanto (the international language invented in 1877) was designed to be a second language that would be easy to learn and easy to speak, making it easier to communicate internationally and thus promote peace. Esperanto still exists and is spoken by about 150,000-300,000 people.

Esperanto has words for chess and all of the chess pieces. It also contains words for chess terms, such as checkmate, stalemate, and perpetual check. For example, "mortigas" is the word for checkmate (to immobilize) and the word for chess is sako (pronounced "shahko")

Although technically not a language, music is sometimes referred to as international. Its notation system is taught worldwide. Musicians can read and play music anywhere in the world.

And that brings us to chess, which also has a notation system and international rules so that the game is played and can be recorded in the same way throughout the planet.

Therefore, at Leisure World there is no need to learn a foreign language to play chess, as in the game pictured in the diagram on the following page. In this game, White is in danger of losing his Queen and the game. What is White's best move?

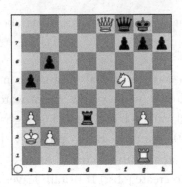

The solution to Puzzle #45 appears on Page 253.

So, do not wait for Esperanto to become more popular. Do not wait for a revival of Latin. Do not wait for a new international language. Play chess now!

Workers Break for National Holiday, But Chess Never Stops

September 6, 2016

Labor Day is the least glamorous of all national holidays. Gifts are not exchanged. Costumes are not worn. Candies are not bought. Fireworks are not shot off. It is generally celebrated simply by taking the day off.

Labor Day marks the end of summer. It is the day after which white clothes cannot or should not be worn until next year. Commercially, it is a good day for selling school supplies.

In the United States, Labor Day is celebrated on the first Monday in September. It recognizes "the dignity of work" and commemorates the contributions of American workers to the economic well-being of the country.

Labor Day developed slowly into a national holiday. It was adopted first by individual municipalities (mainly New York City); then by states (thirty states had adopted it before it became a national holiday by federal law).

The first Labor Day holiday, organized by the Central Labor Union, was celebrated in New York City on a Tuesday in 1882. A second Labor

Day was celebrated there a year later. Twenty thousand working people marched in a parade on Broadway, watched by a quarter million people.

It was a time of labor unrest. Workers in many cities were campaigning and demonstrating for an 8-hour day. Union leaders urged organizations in other cities to follow New York's example to celebrate a "workingmen's holiday." In 1884, labor unions selected the first Monday in September as the day for the holiday. The idea spread so that in the following year, Labor Day was celebrated in numerous industrial centers in the country.

Grover Cleveland (former Governor of New York, an anti-labor President) signed the bill establishing Labor Day as a national holiday in 1894. May 1st (May Day) was specifically avoided as the date for Labor Day because previous celebrations resulted in violence as anarchists and communists joined in worker demonstrations. In many other countries, the labor holiday is celebrated on May Day.

May Day (May 1), originally an agricultural spring festival in Europe, best known for its traditions of dancing around the maypole and crowning the Queen of May, was selected as the day to celebrate International Workers Day, at least partly as a response to the death of workers in the Chicago riot of 1886 in Haymarket Square. It was selected by the socialists and communists of the Second International (a pan-European organization of 20 member countries) at a conference in Brussels in 1891. At least eighty countries around the world celebrate International Workers Day on May 1st.

In Leisure World, the Chess Club does not take a day off, but celebrates the holiday by playing chess. In the game pictured on the following page, both players are even in terms of the number of pieces. Although White's Knight is in jeopardy, White is in a strong offensive position. What is White's best move?

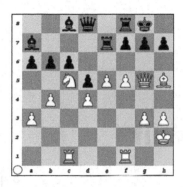

The solution to Puzzle #46 appears on Page 253.

So, do not wait for May Day. Do not wait for a parade down Broadway. Do not wait until the end of next summer. Play chess now!

Do Not Wait

The 50th anniversary of Leisure World would not be complete without a contribution from the Chess Club. The Chess Club is almost as old as Leisure World itself. It has always been looking for new members. The ads in the classified section of Leisure World News and notices on billboards were not enough. So, in recent years, a column was introduced in LW News, commenting on almost any newsworthy or historic event, tying it to chess, and featuring a chess puzzle. At first, the column was read only by chess players, but later drew interest from non-players as well. More than one hundred columns have been published since 2009.

Each column ended with a message, urging readers to "Play chess now!" and not to wait for an excuse to procrastinate--- an excuse that generally was related to whatever was discussed earlier in that column.

For example, in discussing the 200th anniversary of the Congress of Vienna, which ended the Napoleonic era, the column closed with this thought:

"So, do not wait for a large international conference! Do not wait for a horse-drawn carriage or an invitation to the dance! Do not wait for revival of the monarchy! Play chess now!"

In a column, entitled "Is Chess Kosher?" the closing paragraph said: "So, do not wait for a "*hecksher*" [a kosher certification]! Do not wait for government certification! Do not wait for a seal of approval! Play chess now!"

A column on what Americans want in elections ended with: "So, do not wait for the next election! Do not wait for Congress to act! Do not wait for instructions from the American people! Play chess now!"

Further examples imploring readers what not to wait for:

Do not wait for history to repeat itself... the next invasion of the Falkland Islands or the Malvinas... a puff of white smoke from the Vatican... the end of economic sanctions against Iran... a further drop in oil prices ... true energy independence... interplanetary travel ... a decline in world population... lower food prices... more environmental statistics... the return of horse transportation... a French national holiday for Napoleon.

So, do not wait for the next 50th anniversary! Play chess now!

Chess and the English Language

October 7, 2016

The English language has too many words--- more than a million, according to those who count the words, the Global Language Monitor (GLM). To be more exact, as of January 1, 2016, the language has 1,035,877.3 million words, by their count. It will take a lifetime for you to use all those words.

There are about 1.5 billion English-speaking people in the world. Surely, the word supply is large enough to accommodate these speakers. Nobody really knows the size of a college graduate's vocabulary, but some linguists estimate that it is only about 60,000 active words and 75,000 passive words. Who needs more words?

To be exact, the English Language passed the Million Word threshold on June 10, 2009 at 10:22 a.m. (GMT). Currently (as of June 2016), there is a new word created every 98 minutes or about 14.7 words per day. Thus, the English language is growing by over 5,000 words per year or about half of one percentage point a year. Understandably, when a new thing is invented, it needs a name. Emoji and avatar, for example. Hopefully, the word counters will be able to keep up with the growth of neologisms. At least for now, they seem to have a grasp of the magnitude of such growth.

The millionth word was "Web 2.0," a term for the latest generation of web products and services. This is controversial because it contains a number and raises the question: what exactly counts as a word? How are words with multiple meanings counted? Double words? Hyphenated words? Compound words? Slang? Jargon? Proper names and places? Let's find someone to disambiguate this situation.

Using a different approach, other researchers have counted words in the largest dictionaries of various languages. On this basis, English has the most words (171,476 plus 147, 156 obsolete words, and 615,000 definitions). French has only 100,000 and 350,000 definitions.

English has words that describe other words. These include homonyms, antonyms, synonyms, palindrome, onomatopoeia, portmanteau, lexicography, sesquipedalian, and mnemonic.

Many English words come from other languages. That's why we have philologists, who can trace the origin of words and their meanings. These are words, such as dolichocephalic, brachiocephalic, infundibular, and amygdoloidal.

Philologists often fall in love with specific words like retromingent and irredentism. Everyone should use a few favorite, unfamiliar words to shock their friends every once in a while.

Even chess has made contributions to the English language--- words like stalemate and end game, for example. One chess term that is not commonly used in English is a German word: zugzwang (pronounced "tsuk tsuan"). It is a situation where every move left to a player is a bad move, but the player is compelled to move.

In the game pictured on the following page, for example, it is White's turn to move. What is White's best move?

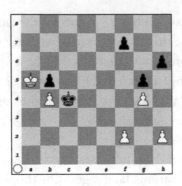

The solution to Puzzle #47 appears on Page 253.

So, do not wait for more neologisms. Do not wait for a dictionary. Do not wait for the English word count to reach two million. Play chess now!

Inching Toward the Metric System

October 21, 2016

As the 40th annual celebration of Metric Week proceeds, it is gratifying to know that the United States is making greater use of the metric system of measurement. Metric Week is always celebrated during the week in which October 10th occurs because it is a system based on tens (the tenth day of the tenth month). It is not celebrated on a date of the Metric calendar because that calendar is not currently in use. (Who would want a ten-day work week anyway?)

The United States is the only industrialized nation that does not *require* use of metrics. Although the system is officially recognized by law here, its use is voluntary. Myanmar (Burma) and Liberia also have not adopted the system.

Use of the metric system has been legal since 1866, when Congress authorized its use and made it unlawful to refuse to trade or deal in metric quantities [Metric Act of 1866 (Public Law 39-183)].

Gradually, over the years, the use of metrics in the United States has been expanding, mostly through Acts of Congress. Following a massive three-year study [Metric Study Act of 1968 (PL 90-472] and further Congressional deliberation, legislation was enacted to increase the use of the metric system in the United States, but without target dates for completion [Metric Conversion Act of 1975 (PL 94-168]. Thus, conversion to metrics essentially is voluntary.

In 1988, Congress bolstered metric conversion by designating metrics as the preferred measurement system, and by requiring each federal agency to use the system in procurement, grants and other business-related activities by the end of fiscal year 1992 [Omnibus Trade and Competitiveness Act of 1988 (Public Law 100-418)]. Many new NASA projects are being designed and built to metric specifications. Most design and construction of Federal Government buildings and facilities are now being done in metric units.

Moreover, since 1994 manufacturers are required to label the net quantity of consumer goods in metrics as well as in U.S. customary units (dual labeling) [Fair Packaging and Labeling Act of 1992 (PL 89-755)]. In addition, attempts are being made to allow labeling in metrics only, equivalent to the requirements existing in the European Union. All States of the United States already have adopted such legislation, except New York and Alabama.

As conversion efforts move ahead, strange consequences are possible. For example, some day the best seats for a football game might be on the 50-meter line. Football and basketball games might be divided into ten periods instead of four and baseball games might be ten innings instead of nine.

Some of our familiar sayings might sound peculiar if updated to metrics. We would have to say: "A miss is as good as 1.6 kilometers." Also, "28.35 grams of prevention is worth 453.59 grams of cure," "A stitch in time saves ten," and "just 5 milliliters (a spoonful) of sugar makes the medicine go down."

This raises questions for chess, too. Will chess convert to metrics and, if so, how? Is it possible to have a ten by ten board instead of eight by eight? Would the number of pieces change from sixteen to ten or twenty? Of course this would revolutionize the game. Leisure Chess Club members, however, are more traditionalists than revolutionaries, as witnessed by the game pictured on the following page.

In this game, Black has just moved the Bishop from b7 to f3, checking the King. What is White's best move?

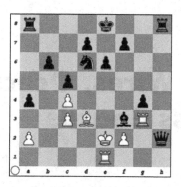

The solution to Puzzle #48 appears on page 253.

So, do not wait for another Act of Congress. Do not wait for Myanmar (Burma) and Liberia to adopt the metric system. Do not wait for the United States to abandon dual labeling requirements. Play chess now!

Crossing Wires, Oceans and Chess Boards

November 4, 2016

October 24th marked the 155th anniversary of completion of the first transcontinental telegraph. Although it is virtually obsolete today, the telegraph was a technical wonder of its day, revolutionizing long-distance communication and helping to unite the east and west coasts of the United States.

Construction of the system was a remarkable feat, considering the conditions faced by the engineers and workers: inclement weather; the need to supply food and materials to the workers at remote locations in unsettled lands; bison knocking over telegraph poles; occasional raids by Native American Indians; potential disruption during the U.S. Civil War; and lack of today's more effective tools, equipment, and building materials.

Demand for better communication was generated by California's population growth following the gold rush in 1848. California's population quadrupled to 380,000 between 1850 (when it became a state) and 1860 (when the Pony Express began). At that time it took at least a month to deliver U.S. mail from New York to San Francisco (by steamship around Cape Horn or through the Isthmus of Panama by mule to a steamship on the Pacific coast). Pony Express reduced the time to about 11 days.

The telegraph could transmit messages rapidly from coast to coast using the electronic dots and dashes of Morse code (named after the inventor,

Samuel F.B. Morse). The code consists of a series of dots and dashes for each letter of the alphabet. An experienced operator could send and receive messages at a rate of 20-30 words per minute.

Pony Express, which operated for only about 18 months, went out of business two days after the transcontinental telegraph system went into operation. Later, the telegraph was outdated by the telephone system, the fax machine, and now the Internet.

In 1841, it had taken 110 days for the news of President Harrison's death to reach Los Angeles. In 1860, California's newspapers received word of Lincoln's election only seven days and 17 hours after the East Coast papers, a big accomplishment at the time.

Computer communications, of course, are much faster and they also are increasing in speed and capacity. It would take 97 minutes to transmit the Encyclopedia Britannica from New York to San Francisco in 1970, according to the Economist magazine, but now the entire contents of the Library of Congress can be sent cross-country in seconds.

Samuel F. B. Morse was a multi-talented man--- an artist as well as an inventor. The son of a Minister, he graduated from Yale, and drew portraits of prominent people, such as the Marquis of Lafayette. He helped launch the New York Journal of Commerce in 1827, and founded the National Academy of Design, where he served as its first president from 1826 to 1845.

He was anti-Catholic and anti-immigrant and twice ran unsuccessfully for Mayor of New York. In 1836, as a candidate of the Native American Party, he received less than 1,500 votes. In 1844, he could not even muster 100 votes.

After his death in 1872, his fame as inventor of the telegraph was obscured by the invention of faster means of communication. He was even overshadowed by Alexander Graham Bell on a series of U.S. commemorative stamps issued in 1940. Morse was pictured on the 2-cent stamp and Bell on the

10-cent stamp. According to one valuation authority, today a Morse stamp in mint condition could fetch 90 cents, whereas Bell's could fetch $17.50.

Nevertheless, Morse is honored with a statue at an entrance to Central Park on Fifth Avenue and 72nd Street. It is untrue that in his last years, he spoke only in Morse code.

Chess players at Leisure World do not need to learn Morse code to play chess. In a recent game (shown here), White has just moved a Pawn to a7, threatening to promote it to a Queen. What is Black's best move?

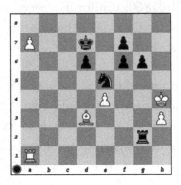

The solution to Puzzle #49 appears on page 254.

So do not wait for a new invention. Do not wait for return of the Pony Express. Do not wait for an SOS distress call. Play chess now!

Horning in on Chess

November 18, 2016

As science marches on, a small startup firm in California has developed a synthetic or bio-fabricated rhinoceros horn, made by copying rhino DNA and using a 3D printer or some other little known, unexplainable process.

The company was attracted to rhino horn by the exorbitantly high price (as much as $150,000 per kilo). It is higher than the price of gold, platinum, or cocaine. The synthetic product could be manufactured and sold for a fraction of that price and still make a profit. The company president contends that sale of the synthetic would bring the market price down far enough to discourage poaching, thereby saving the lives of many rhinos who otherwise would be killed by poachers for their horns.

The price is high and demand is high because users (mostly in Asia) believe that powder from rhino horn is a remedy for all pains, infections, illnesses and diseases. Traditional practitioners of Chinese Medicine believe that rhino powder cures fevers, headaches, hangovers, and even cancers. Some believe it is an aphrodisiac. There is no scientific basis for these beliefs.

Rhino horn has been completely banned from use in medicine in China, Taiwan, and South Korea since 1993. It is no longer listed in medical reference books and is permitted only for research to identify substitutes. In Vietnam, however, rhino horn is widely used for medicinal purposes. It is seen as a symbol of wealth and status by the nouveau riche. Interestingly, rhinos have become extinct in both China and Vietnam.

Poaching has caused a sharp decline in the rhino population, driving the rhino toward extinction. Early in the twentieth century, approximately 500,000 rhinos were prevalent in Africa and Asia. Now they number only about 29,000, mostly in South Africa.

Conservation groups will do almost anything to protect the rhinoceros from poachers, but they are opposed to the marketing and sale of synthetic rhino horns and powder.

Conservationists contend that marketing the synthetic product would tend to increase demand further. New customers would soon want the natural product. Thus, poaching would increase, not diminish. Moreover, law enforcement authorities would have difficulty distinguishing the real product from the synthetic, thereby making it difficult to administer the ban on sales of rhino horn. Wildlife crime is estimated to be worth around $20 billion a year, the third largest criminal industry in the world.

Poachers have become well organized. Poacher gangs use sophisticated methods, including helicopters, drones and night vision equipment to track rhinos, and veterinary drugs to knock them out. To match this level of technology, guards and troops need to be well trained and equipped. Efforts to reduce demand and to combat illegal sales need to become more effective.

Rhinos perform numerous services for the environment. They eat great amounts of grass and bushes, aiding the landscape. They make trails used by other animals. Their dung helps feed fish and birds. Rhino extinction would be a great loss to the ecosystem.

Perhaps the production of synthetic horn is not enough. Science needs to develop hornless rhinos through genetic engineering. Without horns, poachers would be defeated. Rhinos would not be worth hunting and would never become extinct.

While chess players are sympathetic to the plight of the rhinoceros, their games are not affected by potential loss of rhino dung. Games continue unabated at the Leisure World Chess Club, as in the game pictured on the following page.

Black has a better position, but is one Pawn down. It is Black's turn to move. What is Black's best move?

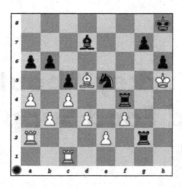

The solution to Puzzle #50 appears on page 254.

So, do not wait for a panacea. Do not wait for synthetic horns. Do not wait for scientists to develop rhinos without horns. Play chess now!

Talking Turkey About the World Food Supply

December 2, 2016

When you celebrate Thanksgiving with a turkey dinner, be thankful that Reverend Malthus was wrong. In 1779, he predicted that the world's population--- probably around 900 million at that time--- would outstrip the world's food supply. Great famine would result, wiping out a large portion of the human population.

Reverend Malthus did not foresee the coming advancements in science, technology, and transportation, which boosted the food supply and distribution system, currently supporting 7 billion people. Although regions of poverty and hunger remain, there has been no general worldwide famine. Modern agriculture is producing more food per capita than ever before.

In fact, the farm animal population now outnumbers the human population by far. The world's average stock of chickens is almost 19 billion, according to statistics from the UN's Food and Agriculture Organization (FAO). Cattle are the next most populous at 1.4 billion, with sheep and pigs at around 1 billion each.

It is hard to count chickens because it is almost impossible to get them to march in single file. Sheep also pose a challenge. Try counting sheep without falling asleep.

China leads the world in the number of chickens, pigs and sheep. The United States has the second largest number of chickens. Brazil and cow-revering India have the greatest number of cattle.

New Zealand and Scotland each have many more sheep than people. New Zealand has 4.4 million people and 30 million sheep; Scotland 5.3 million people and 6.6 million sheep.

Even vegetarians benefit from crop expansion aided by pesticides and genetic modification. In 2013, the world produced roughly 600 million metric tons of fruits and 850 million metric tons of vegetables, according to FAO.

This compilation, of course, violates the admonition "not to add apples and oranges." Apples accounted for 80 million MT of the total; oranges, 70 million MT. Bananas were the largest, however, with over 100 million MT.

Watermelons also produced over 100 million MT, but they are counted as vegetables, not fruits, because they are members of the squash and cucumber family. Tomatoes (164 MT) formed the largest group of vegetables.

There are more than 570 million farms in the world, mainly family farms which produce about 80 percent of the world's food. Agriculture employs over 1.3 billion people throughout the world, or close to 40 percent of the global workforce. In about 50 countries, agriculture employs half of the population and even 75 percent in the poorer nations. Agriculture is the world's largest provider of jobs.

In the United States, 3.2 million farmers operated 2.1 million farms, according to the 2012 Census of Agriculture. The number of U.S. farmers has been declining over the years with fewer farmers producing more food.

With respect to turkeys, the United States reportedly consumes three hundred million turkeys each year, many for Thanksgiving (about 45 million) and Christmas (22 million). Despite the high level of annual consumption, the U.S. and global turkey population remains in the hundreds of millions.

Even during Thanksgiving, chess players do not eat heavily before playing, to avoid digestive distractions.

In the game pictured on this page, it is White's move. Can White avert a checkmate by Black's Queen?

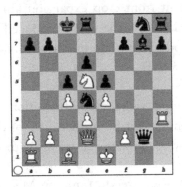

The solution to Puzzle #51 appears on page 254.

So do not wait for next Thanksgiving. Do not wait for humans to outnumber farm animals. Do not wait for exhaustion of the world food supply. Play chess now!

Viva Chess!

December 16, 2016

The recent death of Fidel Castro reminds us that he was a revolutionary and a dictator. He was also a chess player. His brother Raul, now President of Cuba since Fidel stepped down in February 2008, also is a player. Fellow revolutionary Ernesto "Che" Guevara was considered a first class competitor.

Chess is not new to Cuba. In fact, Cuba has one of the strongest chess-playing cultures of any country, dating back to the days of Christopher Columbus. Not only is chess taught in the school system, it is compulsory and is taught at all levels of education, including college. Training at the college level, which began in 2003, has produced around 1,000 chess professors.

The first Cuban championship tournament was held in 1860. Cuba reveres its chess champions, particularly Raul Capablanca who held the world title from 1921-27. A chess club in Havana is named after him and a Capablanca Memorial Tournament is held each year. Cuba has hosted three world championship matches.

During evening hours in Havana, chess games can be seen on the streets under lamppost lights. Cuba has even created postage stamps with chess themes. Four of the seven stamps portrayed a drawing of Capablanca; others pictured a chessboard and chess knights.

Famous U.S. chess player Bobby Fischer competed in the 4th Capablanca Memorial in 1965 by telex from the Marshall Chess Club in New York after being denied a visa by the State Department to compete in person. Fischer's application to visit Cuba as a journalist for the Saturday Review and Chess Life was rejected by passport officials because they did not think a chess tournament was a valid reason to visit a Communist country and because they did not believe Fischer was a bona fide journalist.

In 1966, however, Fischer *was* allowed to compete in the 17th FIDE Chess Olympiad in Havana. Cuba spent over $5 million on that event. Fidel Castro played several exhibition games including a draw with Grandmaster Tigran Petrosian and a win against Bobby Fischer, according to a history written by Bill Wall of chess.com.

Since the Cuban missile crisis of February 1962, the United States has maintained economic sanctions against this island nation of 11 million people. Although travel restrictions have been relaxed in recent years and both countries re-opened embassies in their capital cities in 2015, U.S. economic sanctions remain. Whether relations with Cuba can be fully normalized will depend on policies of newly elected President Trump.

Chess transcends politics. At Leisure World, residents do not need a visa to play chess, nor do they need evidence of chess education in public or private schools. They do not even need to know how to say checkmate in Spanish (jaque mate).

In the game pictured on the following page, White is threatening checkmate at g7 through capture of the Pawn by the Queen. The Pawn, however, is protected by Black's Rook at g8. Black also has an advanced Pawn at a3, which is aspiring to become promoted to Queen. White's Rook, however, is protecting the a1 square. It is White's turn to move. What is White's best move?

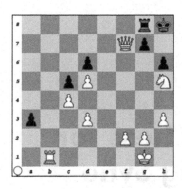

The solution to Puzzle #52 appears on page 254.

So, do not wait for a visa. Do not wait for the end of sanctions against Cuba. Do not wait for capitalism to return to Cuba. Play chess now!

Playing Chess for Auld Lang Syne

January 6, 2017

Television broadcasts showing cities around the world ringing in the New Year may give the impression that New Year's is celebrated on the same day and in the same way in all countries. January 1 in the Gregorian calendar is celebrated widely, but dates vary in many places.

When Emperor Julius Caesar first introduced the Julian calendar in 46 BC, he named January 1 as the first day of the year, honoring Janus, the Roman god of beginnings. Pope Gregory XIII introduced the Gregorian calendar in 1582. The United Kingdom and the United States did not start observing it until 1752.

Some countries observe New Year's Day on January 1 as an official holiday, even though their own national or religious holidays (mostly based on the lunar calendar) occur on other days.

In Korea, Thailand and Vietnam, for example, January 1 is an official national holiday. *Seollal*, the lunar New Year, is also a national holiday in Korea (to be celebrated on January 27 in 2017); in Thailand, *Songkran* is celebrated every April 13; and in Vietnam, *Tet* is to be celebrated on January 27.

Some people in China celebrate New Year's Eve on the last day of December, but the biggest holiday is Chinese New Year, also known as Spring Festival.

It always falls between January 21 and February 20 on the Gregorian calendar. In 2017 (Year of the Rooster), it starts on January 28.

Chinese New Year is celebrated in countries and territories with significant Chinese populations, including Hong Kong, Macau, Taiwan, Singapore, Thailand, Cambodia, Indonesia, Malaysia, Mauritius, and the Philippines, in addition to Mainland China.

Buddhist countries, including Sri Lanka, Cambodia, Myanmar, Thailand, and Laos have extended three-day New Year celebrations, which are celebrated in April. Tibet celebrates in March.

In India, numerous types of New Year's days are celebrated in various regions at various times of the year. For example, Holi is celebrated as New Year's Day in nine of the 29 states, including Madhya Pradesh and Rajasthan. In 2017, Holi begins on the evening of March 12.

In Israel, New Year's Eve is not a national holiday. Jewish New Year, Rosh Hashana, falls between September and October on the Gregorian calendar (in 2017, at sundown on September 20).

Islamic New Year (Hijri) begins on the first day of Muharram, the first month in the Lunar Islamic calendar. In 2017, it starts on the evening of September 21.

In Saudi Arabia, public celebrations of the Gregorian New Year's Eve are banned by the *Committee for the Promotion of Virtue and the Prevention of Vice*, regarded as Saudi Arabia's religious police. Nearby Dubai, however, celebrates on January 1 with gigantic firework displays.

These variations may lead to the question of whether an international agreement is needed to standardize the date and the celebration worldwide. Of course, those who are wedded to tradition would protest if any holidays are lost due to worldwide standardization.

New Year's Eve is celebrated in many ways around the world, not just with parties, champagne, confetti, fireworks and resolutions, but by eating 12 grapes (Spain); burning "moon houses" (Korea); parading with dragons and delivering "red envelopes" (China); visiting families and feasting on family dinners (China, Korea); and by tossing brightly colored powders on friends, relatives, and others (India).

No country, however, celebrates arrival of the New Year with chess games. Many Chess Club members may not be able to resist playing on the holiday. In the game pictured on this page, White has just moved the Pawn to a7, seeking to promote it to a Queen. Can Black prevent it?

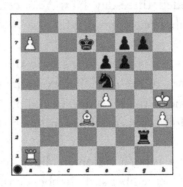

The solution to Puzzle #53 appears on page 254.

So do not wait for a ban on New Year festivities. Do not wait for the date of celebrations to be standardized internationally. Do not wait for integration of the solar and lunar calendars. Play chess now!

Robotic Chess

January 20, 2017

As we learned from the 2016 Presidential election, voters believe that American jobs have been lost because of trade and immigration. However, another culprit is on the rise: robots.

The word "robot" comes from a science fiction play, which premiered on January 25, 1921. By 1923, the word had been translated into thirty languages. The play, written by Karel Capek, was named "R.U.R.," which stands for Rossum's Universal Robots.

A robot (according to the Oxford English Dictionary) is "a machine capable of carrying out a complex series of actions automatically, especially one programmable by a computer."

Optimists believe that robots will change the manner in which work is done and will assist humans in doing their jobs better. The production and servicing of robots will create jobs, including some that do not yet exist. They believe that more jobs will be created than lost, resulting in a net gain in human employment.

Pessimists, on the other hand, believe that just the opposite will happen. Almost any job can be performed by robots and eventually those jobs will become obsolete for humans. For instance, this year 60,000 workers in China were laid off and replaced by robots at the Foxconn factory, which manufactures and assembles cell phones and similar products for Apple, Samsung, and other brands.

Many jobs are vulnerable to replacement by robots. In the medical field, robots already are assisting doctors in performing surgery. In the automobile industry, robots paint cars, install windshields and other parts. Moreover, cars and trucks can now drive themselves through robotic engineering. In hospitals, robots deliver trays of food and drugs, clean linens, and cart away trash. In pharmacies robots dispense drugs and medicines.

Amazon employs 30,000 robots in its distribution centers around the world; and produces its own robots, having acquired Kiva Robotics in 2012 for $775 million.

In Nagasaki, Japan, with a staff of only ten humans, Henn-na Hotel is run almost entirely by robots, some speaking five languages. Yotel in New York City uses robots to handle luggage. In Cupertino, California, Starwood's Aloft Hotel introduced robotic butlers, responsible for delivering amenities to guest rooms, navigating hallways and using elevators without human assistance. Robot bartenders mix and serve drinks on some Royal Caribbean cruise ships.

Eventually, they'll take away all our jobs, except repairing and servicing robots--- at least until we develop a robot that can do that.

Robots are not new to chess enthusiasts, who already play chess against computers. In 1996, a chess-playing computer named "Deep Blue," developed by IBM, won a six-game match against reigning world champion Garry Kasparov.

Chess in Leisure World is not played by robots or computers, only by humans, as illustrated by the diagram on the following page. In this game, Black is ahead in Pawns and has just moved the Queen to c4 to cover the f7 square, thus preventing White's Queen from moving to that square to checkmate the Black King. It is White's turn to move. What is White's best move?

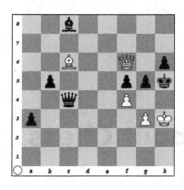

The solution to Puzzle # 54 appears on page 254.

So, do not wait for a robot to take your job. Do not wait for a robot to mix your drinks. Do not wait to converse with a robot in five languages. Play chess now!

Abuzz About Chess

February 3, 2017

Beginning in 2006, bees in many areas began mysteriously disappearing. The phenomenon is called colony collapse disorder, or CCD, and governments have been called in for help. Humans have been collecting honey from bees for about 8,000 years. The bee's major task is to pollinate fruits, vegetables and nuts – about a third of the world's food supply, a market of $40 billion in the U.S. alone.

A bee colony is a marvel of industrial activity and organization that includes division of labor; every bee has a job. A hive usually consists of one queen, thousands of worker bees and hundreds of drones. The queen is the largest and most important; she mates, lays eggs, and keeps the hive in operation for generations.

The female workers care for the queen, feed the colony, build the honeycomb, forage for nectar and pollen and clean and guard the hive. The drones mate with the queen. Queens can live for as long as seven years, while other bees have life spans ranging from a few weeks to six months.

Mating takes place outside the hive in mid-air with about 13-18 drones, one-by-one. The drones die during the act of mating. Afterward, the queen lays her own weight in eggs every couple of hours. She lays about 1,500-2,000 eggs per day; 250,000 eggs each year; and as many as one million in her lifetime.

In response to the CCD crisis, in 2012, the European Union banned certain pesticides (neonicotinoids) thought to pose an "unacceptable" danger to bees. In 2014, the U.S. created an interagency task force to study the situation, but did not ban these pesticides.

Task force scientists are analyzing the key factors impacting pollinator health. Multiple causes of CCD are suspected: mites, pesticides, climate change, and, perhaps, cell phone towers. Mites get into the bees' bloodstream and weaken their immune systems. Pesticides, intended to kill the mites, affect the bees' nervous systems, causing disorientation. Bees forget what they are doing and how to get home.

Climate change may make bees move to warmer areas. Additionally, the animal rights group PETA (People for the Ethical Treatment of Animals) and other ecology advocates believe that overwork, or industrial agriculture, is a cause of CCD. According to this theory, bees are mistreated for the sake of maximizing profits for beekeepers, and are factory-farmed like chickens, pigs and cows.

U.S. beekeepers make most of their money not from selling honey, but from pollinating crops, a business now worth an estimated $10-15 billion annually. Thus, busy bees are caught up in our fast-moving world. They live in cramped quarters, shared with tens of thousands of other bees. They are fed a diet equivalent to junk food. They are transported in trucks and planes by beekeepers to locations far from their native habitats to pollinate crops for clients. One cartoonist mused that if bees earned minimum wages, a jar of honey would cost $180,000.

In chess, as in the beehive, the Queen is most important of all. For example, in the game pictured on the following page, Black has just moved the Pawn to e5, threatening White's Bishop. It is White's turn to move. White can mate in two moves. Do you see it?

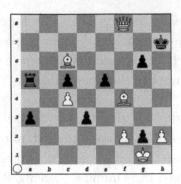

The solution to Puzzle #55 appears on page 255.

So, do not wait for scientific studies. Do not wait for surplus honey. Do not wait for harmless pesticides. Play chess now!

President Trump Plays Chess?

February 17, 2017

Does anyone really know if President Trump plays chess? Some reports in the media have linked Trump and chess. During the Presidential campaign, it was said that Trump was playing chess while all the other candidates were playing checkers or tic-tac-toe. Trump has said on Twitter: "We all know that chess is a game of strategy. So is business."

In describing Trump's skill in attracting media headlines, it was said that "Trump Reminds the World he is Playing 4D Chess on a 3D Chessboard Against People Who Only Know 2D Checkers" No one, however, has reported that the man himself actually plays the game of chess. What is becoming of our journalists?

The Presidential campaign generated a great deal of information about the candidates. The public now knows about each candidate's age, health condition, educational background, work experience, marital status, and income tax bracket. The candidates themselves have tried to explain the knowledge, skills and attributes that would serve them well as President. None of them, however, has mentioned chess-playing as one of their skills.

Chess-playing is not generally recognized as a qualification for becoming President of the United States. Yet more than half of our Presidents (24 of the first 44), including President Obama, have been identified as chess players. The job is so demanding, however, that there is little time for Presidents to actually play a serious game. Perhaps Presidents Day should be set aside to give the President a chance to play a suitable opponent and provide ample photo opportunities for the press.

The White House once released a photo of President Obama firing a shotgun at Camp David. Wouldn't we rather see him playing chess? Perhaps President Trump would play chess with ex-President Obama on Presidents Day, attracting more media attention.

Regardless of the political implications, in honor of President's Day here is a list of Presidents who played chess: George Washington, Thomas Jefferson, James Madison, James Monroe, John Quincy Adams, Andrew Jackson, Martin Van Buren, Millard Fillmore, Abraham Lincoln, Ulysses S. Grant, Rutherford Hayes, James A. Garfield, Grover Cleveland, Theodore Roosevelt, William Howard Taft, Woodrow Wilson, Calvin Coolidge, Franklin D. Roosevelt, Harry S. Truman, Dwight D. Eisenhower, John F. Kennedy, Jimmy Carter, William Jefferson Clinton, and Barack Obama.

The federal government does not regulate chess. Chess sets can be bought and used by anyone, regardless of race, age, gender, or political affiliation. No background check is required. You don't have to be President to play chess at the Leisure World Chess Club. Thus, chess is played regularly at Leisure World, as in the game shown on the following page.

In this game, Black has just moved the Rook to d8 to prevent checkmate. It is White's turn to move. White can win in two moves. Can you see it?

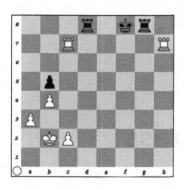

The solution for Puzzle #56 appears on page 255.

So, do not wait for Presidents with chess-playing skills. Do not wait for an Executive Order. Do not wait for regulation of the sale of chess sets by the federal government. Play chess now!

Postal Chess

Forever really isn't forever in the postal service. On January 22, the price of a forever stamp went back up to 49 cents again. The first class rate had been increased on an emergency basis by two cents to 49 cents for a temporary period (January 2014- April 2016) to allow the postal service to recoup $4.6 billion lost during the Great Recession.

The purpose of the latest increase is to generate billions more for the service, which has annual revenues of nearly $70 billion, delivers over 150 billion pieces of mail each year, has $15 billion in debt, and loses money every year ($5.6 billion last year). As former Illinois Senator Everett Dirksen used to say (in his deep voice), "... a billion here, a billion there and soon you're talking about MONEY."

Except for birthday cards and wedding invitations, people just do not want to write messages with pen and paper, and address envelopes by hand, and buy stamps to pay for delivery. They are too busy keeping up with their cell phones, e-mails and social media messages. Meanwhile, the postal service is obliged to deliver mail to 152 million residences from businesses and charities that want your money and are willing to pay for delivery (but not enough).

It is well known that the Postal Service is in financial difficulty. Chess players could be partly responsible for the problem as they no longer play chess by mail. That's a big loss of revenue to USPS. Think of it.

If an average game consists of about 40 moves per person or 80 moves per game, a single game would generate $27.20 in postage at 34 cents per postcard (the current rate). (Remember when they cost only a penny a card?) Multiplied by45 million (the estimated number of chess players in the United States) this would produce roughly $1.2 billion. So, chess correspondence alone could raise more than $2 billion in revenue, if the government could motivate all chess players to play two games per year by mail.

The government needs to find a way to revive chess correspondence. To provide an incentive, the government could establish a million-dollar competition. Players who win the most games or send the most postcards would be awarded a million-dollar prize. The media probably would provide lots of free publicity, as they do for lottery jackpot winnings. Otherwise, the government could use the "health insurance" approach by requiring all chess players to register and to play two games per year by mail or pay a hefty fine.

You won't find players at the Leisure World Chess Club writing postcards to each other. They are busily absorbed in their game, such as the one shown in the accompanying diagram. In this game, Black is cornered and can be checkmated in two moves. It is White's turn to move. Do you see the checkmate?

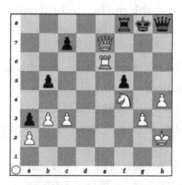

The solution to Puzzle #57 appears on page 255.

So, do not wait for the next postcard! Do not wait to hit the jackpot! Do not wait for postal revenues to balance costs! Play chess "in real time" now!

Italy, Fast Food, and Slow Chess

March 17, 2017

Italians have a love-hate relationship with McDonald's, the fast food chain. Its latest Italian outlet opened in February at Frattocchie, an archaeological site south of Rome. It is a restaurant-museum with a glass walkway, displaying an ancient Roman road and three skeletons. Visitors can enter the museum area without eating at McDonald's, if they so desire.

McDonald's contributed €300,000 (about $315,000) to the project, managed by Rome's agency for Archaeology, Fine Arts and Landscape. The local mayor and the head of McDonald's Italia hailed the project as a "good example of how the public and private sectors can collaborate effectively on reclaiming cultural heritage."

More often, however, McDonald's is seen as a threat to Italian culture. For the past 30 years, Italians have complained that its fast food and golden arches undermine the country's cultural identity. Its first restaurant in Italy, opened near the Spanish steps in Rome in 1986, sparked strong protests.

Thousands rallied to protest the "degradation of Rome" and the "Americanization" of Italian culture; celebrities spoke out against the hazards of fast food. In addition, Valentino, located nearby, sued the chain, maintaining that the foul smell of its fries was ruining the designer's clothes. A long battle ensued, which resulted in McDonald's fixing its venting and airflow.

Despite strong opposition, McDonald's was able to expand its business in Italy. In 1996, McDonald's bought out its competitor, Burghy, a chain owned by Italy's largest meat producer, Gruppo Cremonini. McDonald's took over all 80 Burghy restaurants and in exchange Cremonini became the sole meat supplier for McDonald's in Italy and parts of Europe. McDonald's has grown steadily in the country since then. As of January 2017, it operated 540 McDonald's restaurants, 320 McDrives and 260 McCafés and employed 19, 500 in Italy, mostly in franchises owned by independent local businesses.

At the end of December 2016, despite fierce protests, McDonald's opened its third restaurant near the Vatican, on the ground floor of a Vatican-owned building, which houses seven senior cardinals. Called "McVatican" by some, the restaurant chain pays €30,000 (roughly $33,000) per month rent to the Administration of the Patrimony of the Apostolic See, which manages the Vatican's real estate, according to La Repubblica.

Another protest erupted in July in Florence, when the city rejected a plan for McDonald's to open a fast food outlet at Piazza del Duomo in the heart of the historic city.

McDonald's restaurants are present in about 120 countries. With 36,000 outlets and 1.9 million employees worldwide, not only are its restaurants near the Vatican, and Trevi Fountain, they are located near many other famous tourist attractions, such as the Great Wall of China, the Giza Pyramid in Egypt, the Eiffel Tower and the Louvre in Paris, the Kremlin in Moscow, and Checkpoint Charlie at the Berlin Wall.

There is no McDonald's, however, near the Chess Club in Leisure World. That's just as well because chess players perform better when they are hungry. In the game shown on the following page, it is White's turn to move. White can mate Black in three moves. Do you see it?

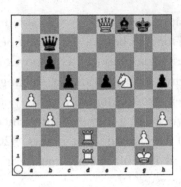

The solution to Puzzle #58 appears on page 255.

So, do not wait for an Italian Big Mac. Do not wait for an archaeological dig. Do not wait for UNESCO to declare Leisure World a historic site. Play chess now!

Chess: Less 'Taxing' Than Doing Your Taxes

April 7, 2017

Historically, taxes were collected even before money was invented. In ancient Egypt, for example, one-fifth of the crops were to be given to Pharaoh. In later years, serfs paid landlords with crops for the land they farmed or with their physical labor.

In ancient Greece, taxes were collected by the military and used to pay for wars. The Greeks and Romans collected taxes from people in colonized territories. Julius Caesar imposed a one-percent sales tax. Property and inheritance taxes were also used.

Religious institutions also collected taxes. Christians paid a tithe or one-tenth of their production, usually paid in kind. Islam charged only one-twentieth of production.

Taxes on commodities became popular. China taxed cooking oil 3,000 years ago. In Russia, Czar Peter the Great taxed beards, beehives, boots, candles, chimneys, hats, horses, nuts, and water. Taxes on salt were popular before refrigeration, as were taxes on whiskey, even after refrigeration.

Early in the history of the United States, the prime source of revenue was a tax or tariff on imports. In 1861, Abraham Lincoln imposed an income tax to finance the Civil War, as collection of duties at southern ports was uncertain at that time. The tax imposed was a flat 3% tax on incomes above $800. In the Revenue Act of 1862, Congress repealed the previous law to end the income tax.

An 1894 law to establish an income tax was declared unconstitutional by the Supreme Court because the tax on dividends, interest, and rents had been deemed to be a direct tax not apportioned by the population of each state. That impediment was removed, however, with ratification of the Sixteenth Amendment to the Constitution in February 1913.

The Revenue Act of 1913 reinstated the federal income tax, presumably to compensate for anticipated lost revenue due to reduction of tariff duties. Originally, tax rates ranged from one percent on income exceeding $3,000 to 7 percent on incomes exceeding $500,000. Since then income tax has become the prime source of government revenue. U.S. tax rates have increased substantially and the tax code has grown phenomenally. In fact, the U.S. tax code is now about 5 times larger than the Bible in terms of word count (3.8 million vs. 0.77 million). It seems almost sacrilegious.

A non-governmental organization reports that since 2001, Congress has made almost 5,000 changes to U.S. tax law. Because income tax is so complex and changeable, almost 60 percent of filers pay someone to prepare their tax returns and 30 percent use commercial software for assistance. According to one estimate, businesses and individuals spend more than 6 billion hours a year to meet tax requirements, the equivalent of 3 million people working full-time annually. (Who says we do not know how to create jobs?)

Residents of Leisure World play chess tax-free. Games are not played for money, just for the pleasure of the game and the intellectual challenge. An example is the game shown in the diagram on the following page. In this game, it is White's turn to move. What is White's best move?

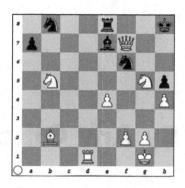

The solution to Puzzle #59 appears on page 255.

So do not wait for tax simplification! Do not wait for an accountant! Do not wait for tax elimination! Play chess now!

A Game By Any Other Name

April 21, 2017

Are names merely labels that distinguish one person from another? Or are they significant in revealing a family's background, its geographic origin, and an ancestor's occupation? Perhaps it could be both.

Juliet, for example, asked: "What's in a name? That which we call a rose by any other name would smell as sweet." Was she saying that Romeo, although a member of a feuding family, did not smell as bad as the other Montagues? She loved him in spite of his name.

Names were simple in the old days. One name per person was enough in ancient Greece. Everybody knew Plato, Socrates, Aristotle, and Herodotus by their first names - - - their only names (mononyms).

Later, however, men in European Mediterranean countries became known by two names: personal or given names, and surnames or family names. Surnames often were based on occupations (Smith, Miller, Shepherd, Baker) or places of birth or residents (Genovese, Romano).

The upper class Romans, though, used three names as a sign of stature: a combination of praenomen (a forename), nomen (a surname), and a cognomen (an additional surname). Thus, Julius Caesar really was Gaius Julius Caesar and Brutus was Marcus Junius Brutus. The lower class plebeians (commoners) had only two names.

Monarchs were known on a first name basis (and with Roman numerals): King George V, King Richard III, and Emperor Napoleon III. Popes get to choose their own names --- different from their birth names. Generally, they choose first names (Pius XIII, Benedict XVI, Francis I), although there are multiple-name exceptions (John Paul I and II).

Some people with multiple names (usually celebrities, actors, entertainers, athletes) want to be known by a single name--- a pseudonym, a stage name, a pen name, a nickname, or an alias.

Thus, they adopt mononyms or pen names: In France, Molière originally was Jean-Baptiste Poquelin; Voltaire was François-Marie Arouet. In the United States, O. Henry (William Sydney Porter); and Mark Twain (Samuel Langhorne Clemens) used pen names.

In the art world, Rembrandt Harmenszoon van Rijn was known as Rembrandt; Michelangelo di Lodovico Buonarroti Simoni was known as Michelangelo; and Doménikos Theotokópoulos was "El Greco."

A number of dictators and authoritarians are known by their surnames: Hirohito, Mussolini, Stalin, Sukarno, and Suharto. Some famous rulers are known by epithets: Peter the Great, and Alexander the Great, for example.

Many in entertainment and sports use single names: Cher, Adele, Madonna, Beyonce, Prince, and Pele; or nicknames: Sting, and Bono.

Criminals had colorful nicknames and aliases: Benjamin "Bugsy" Siegel; Charles "Lucky" Luciano; Alphonse Gabriel "Al" Capone; Meyer Lansky (originally Meier Suchowlanski); Frank Costello (Francesco Castiglia); and Joe Bananas (Joseph Bonanno).

Even chess champion Garry Kasparov originally was named Garik Kimovich Weinstein.

So, what do these names reveal about the persons associated with them? Perhaps the name (or label) makes them more memorable, but does it genuinely indicate the qualities or characteristics of the persons?

You can play chess at Leisure World regardless of your name. You can get involved in games, such as the one pictured on this page. In this game, it is White's turn to move. White can win in two moves. Do you see it?

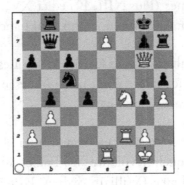

The solution to Puzzle #60 appears on page 255.

So, do not wait for Romeo to marry Juliet. Do not wait for a pseudonym. Do not wait for a name with a Roman number. Play chess now!

Chess Toadies Leap Into the Game

May 5, 2017

The world is facing another crisis. It has been known since the 1980s that the population of frogs, toads, and amphibians is decreasing, but recently the rate of decline has accelerated.

Roughly 6,800 species of frogs inhabit the earth. About one-third of them are considered endangered. Much of the decline is attributed to deforestation and climate change, but also to pollution, pesticides, ozone depletion, ultraviolet radiation, disease, predators, and even increased noise levels (which interfere with mating calls).

Many species around the world have been identified as "critically endangered," a serious threat to global diversity. You just know frogs are in trouble when an organization is created, named "SAVE THE FROGS."

Yes, there is such an organization. In fact, on April 29 it celebrated its Ninth Annual "Save the Frogs Day." It is "the world's largest day of amphibian education and conservation action," according to the organization. You may have missed it. It was an opportunity to party or parade or to attend an educational seminar on frogs. You could have learned the difference between frogs and toads.

Toads generally have shorter legs, have rougher skin, and lay eggs in a string-like structure rather than in a grape-like bunch. However, some frogs may have skin covered in warts, and some toads may have smooth, slimy skin, according to a San Francisco science museum. So, it is often hard to tell the difference, unless you check out their eggs. (This may seem trivial, but it is important to the frogs and toads, especially during mating season.)

You might also have learned that some frogs are poisonous, such as the poison dart frog, which is an endangered species. A small drop of poison can kill you in three minutes. There is no antidote. A single frog can hold enough poison to kill ten men. These frogs are hard to find because they are small (0.5-2 inches long) and live in tropical rainforests, but they are brightly colored and patterned.

Brilliantly colored frogs are popular with pet collectors in the United States and Europe, who buy them from smugglers in South and Central America. Encouraged by high demand and high prices in the international pet trade, smugglers often hide the little creatures in luggage, or conceal them in legal shipments of exported tropical fish. Customs officials estimate that close to 90 percent of illegally exported poison dart frogs die in transport because of poor shipping conditions.

Numerous species of frogs are listed as endangered by the International Union for Conservation of Nature (IUCN), an organization that tries to raise awareness and protect endangered species; and by the Convention on International Trade in Endangered Species of Wild Fauna and Flora (CITES), a multilateral treaty to protect endangered plants and animals.

In Colombia and some other nearby countries, wildlife conservation areas have been set up in order to protect such endangered species.

If so inclined, you can join an ecology tour in Costa Rica, sponsored by SAVE THE FROGS, July 14-25, 2017. Costa Rica is home to 202 known species of amphibians.

For chess players, frogs are a distraction. Fortunately, Clubhouse II does not permit frogs to enter. When is the last time you saw frogs in the clubhouse?

Chess players are not easily distracted, as in the game pictured on this page. In this game, White is threatening to promote a Pawn to Queen on b7. However, it is Black's turn to move. What is Black's best move?

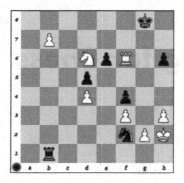

The solution to Puzzle #61 appears on page 255.

So, do not wait for frog extinction! Do not wait for an ecology tour! Do not wait for mating season! Play chess now!

Exercising for Chess

May 19, 2017

In preparing for tournaments, some avid chess players engage in vigorous physical workouts to relieve tension and to clear their minds for the competition. Since many of you may not have visited the gym for a while, here are some chess exercises that can be done safely at home.

- Sit at the dining room table. Place your left elbow on the table. Make a fist with that hand. Place your cheek on the fist. Sit this way for 45 minutes. If anyone walks in, they will wonder what you are doing. Ignore them.
- A variation is to place both elbows on the table. Cup your hands. Place your chin in the cup. Maintain this position for 45 minutes. This variation saves you from having to make a fist.
- Another way you can prepare for chess is to lie on the floor somewhere. Roll over on your right side. Move your knees toward your chest in a fetal position. Relax until you fall asleep. Repeat nightly. For variety, you can roll onto your left side at times.

Patience is a virtue, especially when it takes a long time to complete a chess game. The longest game on record in terms of moves, took place in 1989 in Belgrade. Ivan Nicolaic played Goran Arsovic for 20 hours and 15 minutes, making 269 moves. The game ended in a draw. The longest game in terms of time, took place in Israel in 1980. Yadael Stepak beat Yaakov Mashina in 24 hours and 30 minutes, after 193 moves.

Waiting for your opponent to make a move can be exasperating, but it need not be. You can put the time to good use and sharpen your physical and mental capacity by performing exercises while waiting for the next move. Here are a few examples.

- While your adversary is focusing on the chessboard, quietly get out of your chair and walk behind it. Raise one leg off the ground and to the side. Hold this position for ten seconds and repeat the exercise with your other leg. This is a good warm-up. Then place your hands on the back of the chair. Lift both feet off the ground and do a handstand. Visualize a scene in which you are doing this on the parallel bars in Olympic competition. Hold it as long as you can. Then return to the ground and sit down quietly. By this time, your opponent may have made a move.
- Another suggestion is to change positions on the chair. Instead of sitting on it, stand on it. Fold your arms across your chest, crouch down and kick your feet one at a time, as if you were doing a Russian "Kozatsky" dance. As you perform this exercise, think of the fast music that would accompany this Cossack dance at a wedding. Continue the exercise until the music stops. (Caution: Do not try this at home.) Then sit down casually and resume playing. By this time your opponent may have made a move.

Granted, these are difficult exercises, but if you can accomplish them, they are guaranteed to spook the hell out of your opponent.

This rarely happens during chess games. If you wander into the clubhouse and see these exercises being performed, you are in the wrong place. You are in the gym, not the lobby.

In the game shown on the following page, White is threatening to promote the Pawn at c7 to a Queen. It is Black's turn to move. What is Black's best move?

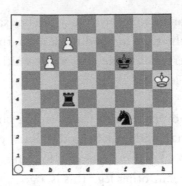

The solution to Puzzle #62 appears on page 255.

So, do not wait for the perfect exercise to prepare for chess. Do not wait for your opponent to move quickly. Do not wait for a Cossack dance. Play chess now!

Chess: a Socially Sanctioned Love Affair

June 2, 2017

General Petraeus is back in the news again. In February he testified before the House Armed Services Committee on threats to world order. The retired 4-star general, you will recall, resigned as Director of the Central Intelligence Agency (CIA) about five years ago because of a scandalous affair with Paula Broadwell, his biographer. He should have played chess instead.

Petraeus served over 37 years in the U.S. military, including command of coalition forces in Iraq and Afghanistan. He graduated with distinction from the U.S. Military Academy and earned M.P.A. and Ph.D. degrees from Princeton University and is currently affiliated with three universities (CUNY, USC, Harvard). He is the recipient of numerous U.S., NATO and UN medals and awards, and decorations from 13 foreign countries.

While attending the U.S. Military Academy at West Point, David Petraeus met Hollister ("Holly") Knowlton on a blind date. She is the daughter of General William A. Knowlton, who was Superintendant of the Academy at the time. The couple married on May 12, 1974. Mrs. Petraeus worked in jobs providing consumer education and advocacy for military personnel and their families. She retired in January 2017 from the Consumer Finance Protection Bureau (starting annual salary $187,605). She and her two children never spoke publicly about her husband's affair.

In May 2013, David Petraeus became a partner in Kohlberg Kravis Roberts & Co. L.P. (KKR), a New York investment firm, and chairman of the firm's newly created KKR Global Institute. In July 2013, Petraeus was named a visiting professor at the City University of New York. He was to be paid $200,000 to deliver a three-hour weekly seminar. Full-time professors and adjuncts earn far less at CUNY for teaching a full load of classes. After city and state officials criticized the high pay, Petraeus agreed to take the position for just $1.

Paula Broadwell, 20 years younger than Petraeus, served on active and reserve army duty for over 20 years. In her home town, Bismarck, North Dakota, she was homecoming queen, valedictorian, and an All-State basketball player. She earned a Bachelor degree from West Point and a Master of Arts degree from the University of Denver. A New York Times article quoted sources, describing her as an "ambitious overachiever;" an "Olympic-distance triathlete" who could run a 6-minute mile; "curvaceous," with "expressive green eyes;" and "seemingly immune to the notion of modesty."

With Vernon Loeb, she co-authored a biography of Petraeus, published in January 2012. She remains married to Dr. Scott Broadwell, whom she met when they both were captains in the U.S. Army. They have two sons. She is best known for her extramarital affair with then-CIA director, David Petraeus.

As fallout from the affair, Petraeus resigned from the CIA and later pleaded guilty to a misdemeanor charge of mishandling classified material. He was sentenced to two years' probation and a $100,000 fine. It is not true that he had to wear a scarlet letter A alongside his service ribbons. Mrs. Broadwell was never charged. However, she lost her security clearance and her promotion to Lieutenant Colonel.

Chess is available everywhere, even in Afghanistan. Chess is ethical, moral, and socially acceptable. You cannot be blackmailed for playing chess. To fill his spare time, Petraeus could have played chess.

What happened to General Petraeus has not happened at Leisure World because there is a Chess Club. Witness the diagram on this page. Black pieces outnumber White, but it is White's turn to move. What is White's best move?

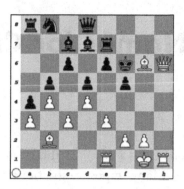

The solution to Puzzle #63 appears on Page 255.

So, do not wait for a biographer. Do not wait for more intelligence. Do not wait for a scarlet letter. Play chess now!

No Bad Names for Chess

June 16, 2017

Government regulation begins at birth. In this country, State governments regulate baby naming. Many impose restrictions to avoid objectionable names, to protect the child from embarrassment or harm in later life, and for various other reasons. Many state restrictions are based on technological needs--- assuring that names are compatible with computer systems.

Thus, several states (e.g., California, Massachusetts, New York, Texas) explicitly limit the number of characters in a name. Some require use of the English alphabet only, excluding numerals, symbols, pictographs, ideograms and diacritical marks (California, Texas, New Jersey). In New Jersey, numbers are permitted as names if they are spelled out (Eightyfive, Ochocinco). In Texas, roman numerals are allowed, but not arabic (James Addison Baker III, not James Addison Baker 3). Some states, however, have no restrictions at all (Delaware, Kentucky, Maryland, Montana).

Other countries have more restrictive naming laws. In Iceland, for example, parents must choose from a list of 1,853 female names and 1,712 male names. Also, the Icelandic alphabet must be used. Names like Charles and Carol are not recognized because there is no "c" in the Icelandic alphabet.

Parents in Denmark must draw from a list of 7,000 pre-approved names. Portugal has an 80-page list with about 2,000 banned names; the Mexican state of Sonora, 60; New Zealand, more than 100. In Norway, one mother was sent to jail for failure to pay a $420 fine for using an unapproved name (Gesher).

In Germany, surnames cannot be used as first names (e.g. Schroeder, Kohl), nor can names of objects or products. Osama Bin Laden was rejected because it is not consistent with German naming guidelines and is illegal in the parents' home country (Turkey).

In China (with a language of tens of thousands of characters), parents are required to choose names with characters that computer scanners can read, particularly for national identification cards. Numbers and non-Chinese symbols and characters are not allowed.

In Japan, only official "kanji" (Chinese letters or characters) may be used. The purpose is to assure that all names can be easily read and written by the Japanese. Local authorities can reject names deemed to be inappropriate. Akuma (devil) is an example.

In Malaysia, parents cannot name children "Woti," which means "sexual intercourse" or Chow Tow ("Smelly Head"), nor can they use names of animals, insects, fruits, vegetables, or colors.

On Morocco's list of approved names, a baby can be named "Sara" (Arabic version), but not "Sarah" (Hebrew version). In 2009, human rights groups charged the Moroccan government with ethnic discrimination for not allowing Berber (a.k.a. Amazigh) parents to choose Amazigh names for their babies. Morocco claimed those names were rejected because they "contradict the Moroccan identity." In the past, the Amazigh language had been criminalized in Morocco.

Saudi Arabia banned 50 names deemed to be "blasphemous," "foreign," or "politically controversial," including Linda, Elaine, Sandy, Alice, and Lauren, as well as Binyamin (the first name of Israel's prime minister).

More names specifically banned include: Superman (Sweden); Batman (Sonora State, Mexico); Mona Lisa (Portugal); Anus (Denmark); Lady Di, (Sonora State, Mexico); Sex Fruit (New Zealand); and Adolf Hitler (Germany, Malaysia, New Zealand).

Regardless of your name or your children's names, you can play chess at Leisure World. In the game shown on this page, it is Black's turn to move. What is Black's best move?

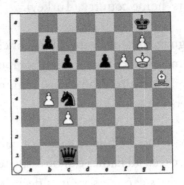

The solution to Puzzle# 64 appears on Page 256.

So do not wait for a birth certificate. Do not wait for a banned name. Do not wait for government approval. Play chess now!

Going Bananas Over Chess

July 7, 2017

The world has too many crises: national security crises, missile and defense crises, immigration crises, drug crises, environmental crises, and financial crises. Many books have been written about crisis management. Crises are becoming commonplace. No wonder there is complacency about the banana crisis.

The banana crisis has been known for a long time. In the 1950s, fusarium fungus ("Panama Disease") wiped out the entire Gros Michel ("Big Mike") variety. The fungus lives in the soil and attacks banana plants at the roots, causing them to rot from the inside.

The Gros Michel was replaced by the Cavendish variety, which originally was immune to the disease. However, the current fungus strain now attacks Cavendish and has affected banana crops stretching from Southeast Asia to Australia, Africa and the Middle East. Fear is that it will soon strike Latin America, which produces large quantities for export, almost entirely the Cavendish variety.

Scientists are at work to save the $36 billion industry. They have developed better ways to detect and track the fungus; herbicides to eradicate pests to the banana plant (some plantations are sprayed aerially as much as 50 times a year); and irradiation to destroy fungi. Through genetic engineering, the ultimate goal is to develop a mutant super banana completely resistant to fungal diseases.

Although bananas have existed for thousands of years, the first banana did not arrive in the United States until 1876, when it was introduced at the World's Fair in Philadelphia's Fairmont Park. In those early days, the banana was a delicacy, selling for 10 cents apiece, often wrapped in tinfoil and eaten with a knife and fork, according to a daily website (famousdaily.com).

Today, Americans eat more bananas than any other fruit--- more than apples and oranges combined. More than 100 billion bananas are consumed annually in the world. 85% of the world's banana production is used for local consumption, and only 15% is exported (mainly to the United States and Europe). 17 million tons of bananas are exported globally each year, almost all of which are Cavendish. Ecuador is the world's largest exporter of bananas.

Contrary to general belief, bananas do not grow on trees. They grow as a plant in the ground. Bananas do not hang down from branches; they grow upward, defying gravity. Banana plants can grow up to 30 feet high without woody trunks.

Bananas are a healthy source of fiber, potassium, vitamin B6, vitamin C, and various antioxidants (substances that prevent cell damage caused by oxidation in the body) and phytonutrients (natural chemicals that may help prevent disease). Thus, bananas promote normal blood pressure and regularity of bowel function, contributing to heart and digestive health.

Unfortunately, while scientists search for solutions to banana diseases, America's most popular fruit remains in danger of extinction.

Chess players at Leisure World are well accustomed to crises. Each game is a crisis. For example in the game shown on the following page, White's Queen is threatened by Black's Knight at c6 and also by Black's Queen at d8. However, it is White's turn to move. What is White's best move? (Note: there are two solutions.)

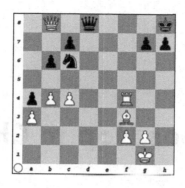

The solution to Puzzle #65 appears on page 256.

So, do not wait for the next crisis! Do not wait for bananas to ripen! Do not wait for a banana shortage! Play chess now!

Kangaroos Hop to Chess

July 21, 2017

Despite all the real estate in the world, kangaroos live only in Australia and Tasmania. They have been there for many thousands of years. Unlike many other animals living in the wild, kangaroos are not endangered with extinction (except for the Tasmanian forester kangaroo). The International Union for Conservation in Nature (IUCN), an international organization that monitors endangered species worldwide, considers them "of least concern."

In a country of about 25 million, kangaroos outnumber the human population. The kangaroo population has been estimated at 50-60 million in some years, according to Australia's census for commercially harvested kangaroos. At that rate, the country would have twice as many kangaroos as people. Kangaroos also outnumber cattle (28.7 million), but not sheep (about 74 million).

Kangaroos cannot walk. They can only hop and they can only hop forward, not backward. Also, they do not have thumbs. They get around using their big, powerful hind legs to hop wherever they want to go. In fact, kangaroos can travel at speeds up to 30 miles per hour and can leap 30 feet. They also use their muscular tails to help keep their balance. Fully-grown kangaroos are usually 5-6 feet tall and weigh 50-120 pounds.

Females are burdened with pockets or pouches, designed to carry their babies for about eight months until they are ready to live on their own. The babies are particularly small at birth--- about the size of a cherry. They are born at a very immature stage, weighing less than a gram and measuring only about 2 cm long. A baby kangaroo, called a joey, lives in the pouch and feeds on the mother's milk. Males do not have pouches, nor do they have milk--- a shining example of gender inequality in nature.

Kangaroos live in groups of ten or more, known as "mobs." Females mate with the dominant male, usually the oldest and biggest of the mob. They are herbivores and can survive for long periods without water.

Human consumption of kangaroo meat became legal in South Australia in 1980; it did not become legal throughout all of Australia until 1993. The meat can be prepared as stir fries, leg roasts, steaks, meatballs, kebabs and sausages. The tail can be used for soup. If not overcooked, the meat is tender and has a beefy, slightly sweet and smoky flavor.

Kangatarians (vegetarians who eat only kangaroo meat) regard it as a healthy food--- extremely lean, low in saturated fats, full of iron, free-range and organic. Kangaroos are well suited for kangatarians, who are seriously concerned about the environment and ethics. They produce a lower level of greenhouse gas emissions than cattle; they require no additional feed, water or land cleared for them; they can roam more freely and are slaughtered more humanely than farm animals.

In Muslim countries, kangaroo meat is considered halal, according to a fatwa issued by Turkey's Religious Affairs Directorate (Diyanet). However, the meat is not kosher inasmuch as kangaroos do not chew their cud and do not have cloven hooves.

Chess players admire the freedom of movement of kangaroos. As they play the game, they seek to gain mobility for their own chess pieces and to create restrictions for their opponents'.

In the diagram on the following page, White is threatening to promote the Pawn on b7 to a Queen. It is Black's turn to move. What is Black's best move?

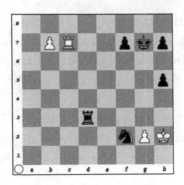

The solution to Puzzle #66 appears on Page 256.

So, do not wait for kangaroo extinction. Do not wait for kangaroos to hop backwards. Do not wait for kosher kangaroos. Play chess now!

No Vacation From Chess

August 4, 2017

Seemingly, nothing ever happens in August. Everybody goes on vacation. In European countries, governments close down for the full month. In Rome, the local population goes elsewhere and leaves the city entirely to tourists. It is a slow, hot month.

In the United States, August is a slow-news month. Congress is not in session. There are no national holidays to celebrate. It is too hot for Halloween costumes, Valentine candies, Easter eggs and even for Santa Claus. It is too hot for serious work.

It is time for vacation; time for immersing oneself in water at beaches and swimming pools to cool down; time for smearing one's body with lotions to protect against the sun.

August is a quiet month. "Vacation" itself is a quiet word. It comes from the Latin word *vacare*, which means free or open. So we get the words *vacate*, *vacant*, *vacuum* and *vacation*. (Where would English be without Latin?)

In the original Roman calendar the month of August was called Sextilis because it was the sixth month of the year. After January and February were added to the calendar, it became the eighth month of the year. At that time, the month had only 29 days. Two days were added, however, when Julius Caesar created the Julian calendar in 45 BC, giving the month 31 days. The month was later renamed Augustus in honor of the first emperor of Rome, Caesar Augustus and to recognize that many of his greatest triumphs occurred during the month.

Some historic events did take place in August. Most notable were the beginning of World War I (1914) and the dropping of atomic bombs on Japan toward the end of World War II (1945). Joseph Priestley discovered oxygen (1774). Christopher Columbus sailed from Spain (1492). Thomas Edison patented the kinetograph (camera) (1897). Mona Lisa was stolen from the Louvre (1911) (and was recovered two years later). The first telegraph message to circle the earth was sent by the New York Times (1911). Hawaii became the 50th State (1959). The Berlin Wall came into existence (1961). Martin Luther King made his "I Have a Dream" speech in Washington, DC (1963).

Throughout history, many famous people were born in August, including King Louis XVI, Napoleon Bonaparte, Fidel Castro, Queen Elizabeth, and Mother Theresa. Also born in August were Orville Wright, both explorers Lewis and Clark (William Clark and Meriwether Lewis); former U.S. Presidents Benjamin Harrison, Herbert Hoover, Lyndon Johnson, William Clinton, and Barack Obama; Senator John McCain and many celebrities from sports (Cal Ripken, Ted Williams, Roger Federer, Sonny Jurgensen), entertainment (Leonard Bernstein, Claude Debussy, Charles Boyer, Ingrid Bergman), literature (Leo Tolstoy, Herman Melville, Alex Haley) and business (Warren Buffett, Malcolm Forbes, Steve Case, George Soros).

Some famous people also died in August: Marilyn Monroe, Elvis Presley, Babe Ruth, Neil Armstrong, Truman Capote, Alexander Graham Bell, Andrew Carnegie, Warren Harding, and Princess Diana.

In Leisure World, it is not too hot to play chess in August. Chess is played regularly in the air- conditioned comfort of Clubhouse II. In the game on the following page, it is White's turn to move. What is White's best move?

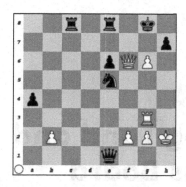

The solution to Puzzle# 67 appears on Page 256.

So, do not wait for the summer heat to subside! Do not wait for a more eventful August! Do not wait for the end of vacation! Play chess now!

Surveying Land and the Chess Board

August 18, 2017

Two men worked methodically for five years to create the Mason-Dixon Line, setting the border between Maryland and Pennsylvania. The line, perhaps the most famous boundary in the world and subsequently a symbolic separation between "free states" and "slave states," is named for them. A remarkable technical accomplishment for its time, the job probably could have been completed in five seconds with today's technology. If only they could have waited for the Global Positioning System (GPS) and Google Maps.

This raises questions. Why could they not wait? Why did it take five years? How did these two men do it? Did they work in the wilderness? Did they camp out each night? What did they do for food and water?

They couldn't wait because there was a pressing need for a survey to resolve an 80-year old dispute between the two colonies. After local surveyors failed to draw the line, Thomas Penn and Frederick Calvert (also known as Lord Baltimore) asked the Royal Society in England for help.

The society recommended Charles Mason (an astronomer) and Jeremiah Dixon (a surveyor) for the job. In November 1763, they left Britain and arrived in Philadelphia with many tools and equipment, including: a zenith sector; a set of star tables prepared by the Royal Observatory; and 200 stone pillars, each weighing at least 400 pounds, to be used as mileage markers. The zenith sector, a very accurate six-foot telescope, one-quarter of the size of the Observatory's instrument, was built especially for the task.

In Philadelphia, they added a specially made pendulum clock to time their astronomical observations. They would make multiple observations of five different stars to determine the latitude, then travel west to find another point with exactly the same latitude. This would continue for five years, marking individual points and surveying to mark straight lines between them.

With all the equipment they hauled, it was clear they could not do the job alone. In those days before interstate highways and roadside motels, they needed help--- guides, horses, wagons, and workers to clear trees and foliage and to move the heavy stone markers. They needed interpreters to deal with Native American Indians.

They cut a 24-foot-wide path through the dense woods, the mountains, and valleys. Every mile was marked by stones and by crown stones every 5 miles. They crossed rivers and moved west about 2 miles a day, along with as many as 120 people at a time, including 40 ax men, a herd of sheep and a milkmaid.

Mason and Dixon completed their work in October 1767, having surveyed 233 miles, ending just northwest of Oakland, Maryland. They installed 133 stone markers along the line, many of which were lost over time. Ironically, GPS technology was used later to find the lost stones.

Geography is no obstacle to chess. It can be played north or south of the Mason-Dixon Line. In the illustrated game on the following page, White has an advantage in manpower. How can it best be used?

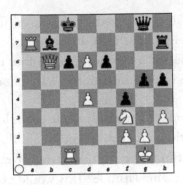

The solution to Puzzle #68 appears on Page 256.

So, do not wait for further measurements. Do not wait for more milestone markers. Do not wait for technological advancements. Play chess now!

Jobs for Labor Day

September 1, 2017

Labor Day is almost here, reminding us of the economic and political need to create jobs for American workers. The holiday is celebrated mostly by people who have jobs. They celebrate by not working--- taking the day off. Those without jobs have no cause to celebrate. Today, nearly one-quarter million are collecting unemployment and many other jobless workers have exhausted their unemployment compensation. The situation is critical in some locations.

Job creation as a result of economic growth is considered desirable, whereas the very essence of business is to make profits by cutting costs to increase productivity and efficiency; to produce more output with the same or fewer workers. It is one of the great contradictions of our times. Nevertheless, politicians all seem to favor job creation because that is what the voters want.

One way to increase employment is to bring back the old jobs that are long gone, but not forgotten. Many of our jobs have been taken away by self-service. What can be done to bring back those lost jobs?

For example, drivers should not be allowed to pump their own gasoline, thereby creating jobs for service station attendants (as in New Jersey). Office buildings should be required to hire elevator operators and each elevator should be required to have an engineer on board in case of breakdowns. Sales people should be readily available at department stores to show you what merchandise is available and tell you what it costs. Automatic teller machines should be banned so that more bank clerks will be hired.

Wheeled luggage should not be allowed in hotels and bell hops should be required to show you to your room. Bowling alleys should hire pin setters, a good job for youngsters. Restaurants should not offer salad bars or buffet meals so that more servers will be hired.

Research on driverless vehicles should be halted and eighteen wheelers should be required to have two truck drivers, one to sleep while the other drives. Horse transportation would bring back blacksmiths and street cleaners, who could sell the manure by-product to farmers for fertilizer. Icemen in horse-drawn wagons could deliver blocks of ice to help preserve food if your refrigerator does not work.

New York, London and other cities employed thousands of people to work as lamplighters, a respectable job that was passed down from father to son. Town criers were used to police the area and present the news at 11 pm. "Eleven pm and all's well," they cried. That's all we need to know.

These are service jobs that cannot be shifted easily to China or other low wage countries

How will we pay for all these returning jobs? Politicians will tell us that the increase in employment and purchasing power, along with tax cuts and unemployment savings, will stimulate the economy, generating more revenue. Thus, the system will pay for itself.

As a result, more workers will be able to celebrate Labor Day as a day of rest. Chess players at Leisure World do not take a day off. They celebrate Labor Day by playing chess.

In the game pictured on the following page, White's King has just moved from c5 to d4 to get out of check. What is Black's best move?

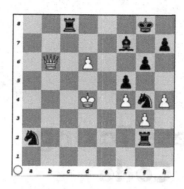

The solution to Puzzle #69 appears on Page 256.

So, do not wait for the end of self-service. Do not throw away your wheeled luggage. Do not wait for the ice man. Play chess now!

Chess: Less Taxing
than Tax Code

September 15, 2017

It is tax time again for those who file estimated quarterly taxes.

Many taxpayers dread calculating and filling out tax forms more than they dread paying the taxes. They should be relieved to know, however, that there are over a million tax preparers in the United States ready to help.

There are more tax preparers in the country than firefighters and policemen combined, according to a research project ("Face the Facts USA") based at George Washington University: 1.2 million tax preparers compared to 310,400 firemen and 765,000 police. The number of firemen and police are understated, but the point is well made--- the U.S. tax code is extremely complicated and generates lots of work.

Evidently, the study counted only the career firefighters, and not the volunteers. Also, it counted only the full-time state and local police officers who could make arrests, not the unsworn, the part-time, and the federal police.

The total number of firemen alone exceeded one million in 2015, according to estimates of the National Fire Protection Association (345,600 career firefighters; 814,850 volunteers).

The number of state and local police also exceeded one million, including 765,000 sworn officers with general arrest powers. Agencies also employed approximately 100,000 part-time employees, including 44,000 sworn officers. In addition, the federal government employed 120,000 full-time law enforcement officers, authorized to make arrests and carry firearms.

In any event, the tax code is notoriously complicated and cumbersome. Federal tax law has grown from just 400 pages in 1913, to more than 72,000 pages today. The tax code is 3.8 million words long, nearly 5 times longer than the Bible. It is also 4 times larger than the combined works of William Shakespeare. Jay Leno once said: "… if Romeo and Juliet were alive today and tried to do a joint return, they'd probably kill themselves again."

A non-governmental organization reports that since 2001, Congress has made about 5,000 changes to U.S. tax law. Because income tax is so complex and changeable, almost 60 percent of filers pay someone to prepare their tax returns and 30 percent use commercial software for assistance (e.g., Turbotax), according to the Internal Revenue Service (IRS). American businesses and individuals spend more than 6 billion hours a year to meet tax requirements, the equivalent of 3 million people working full-time, year-round. The IRS itself employs 90,000 workers.

Much effort around the world goes into tax collection, but you can escape income tax if you move your permanent residence to one of the following places, where there is no income tax: The Bahamas, Bahrain, Bermuda, Cayman Islands, Hong Kong, Kuwait, Monaco, Oman, Qatar, Saudi Arabia, and United Arab Emirates.

Chess can be played anywhere and chess rules are less complicated than the tax code. In the game pictured on the following page, both sides have two rooks, but Black has a Pawn as well. It is Black's turn to move. What is Black's best move?

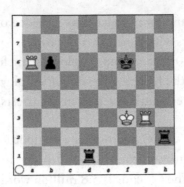

The solution to Puzzle #70 appears on page 256.

So, do not wait for more tax changes. Do not wait for a permanent change of residence. Do not wait for tax help from firefighters or police. Play chess now!

Border Disputes

October 6, 2017

Philadelphia would be part of Maryland if the Mason-Dixon Line had gone directly across the 40th parallel to the Atlantic coast, which is north of present-day Philadelphia. While the line generally follows the 40th parallel from west to east, at a point not too far from Philadelphia it turns in a north-south direction to form what is now the 83-mile boundary between Maryland and Delaware.

During negotiations in 1732, Maryland "tried to hold out for the 40th parallel, but Pennsylvania colonists had settled enough land to the west and southward of Philadelphia that this was no longer practical," according to a history of the Mason-Dixon Line by John Mackenzie of the University of Delaware.

The survey by Charles Mason and Jeremiah Dixon of England's Royal Society, which began in 1763, helped to settle an 80-year dispute over the border between the two colonies. It was instrumental in forming part of the borders between Maryland, Pennsylvania, Delaware and West Virginia. The project stopped in the southwest corner of Pennsylvania, 22 miles short of its destination, because of the war among Indian tribes in that territory.

Mason was 35 when the survey started; Dixon, 30. After completion, both returned to England. Dixon never returned to America. He died unmarried at the age of 45 and is buried in an unmarked grave in Quaker cemetery in Staindrop County, Durham, England.

Mason returned to Philadelphia in 1786 with his second wife, 7 sons and a daughter. He died there and is buried in Christ Church Burial Ground, the final resting place of many dignitaries, including Benjamin Franklin.

It is not clear how much was paid for the original survey. According to Encyclopedia Britannica, the cost of drawing the line was $75,000. According to a 1975 New York Times article, "Mason and Dixon took 5 years…and were paid $16,000." A history by the town of Rising Sun, Maryland states that "It cost the Calverts of Maryland and the Penns of Pennsylvania £3,512/9 s…" for the 244-mile survey. How much is that in today's American money?

When a project takes 5 years for completion, its anniversaries can be celebrated based on the opening date, the closing date, or during all 5 years. Thus, celebrations of the 250th anniversary of the line began in 2013, coinciding with the start of the land survey. Celebrations at various locations will end this October, commemorating completion of the project.

Historic reenactments will be held at Mason-Dixon Historical Park in Core, West Virginia (about 60 miles south of what is now Pittsburgh), along with walks, speakers, craft shows, food and music. On the Pennsylvania side highlights will include guided walks into Greene County and to the marker atop Brown's Hill, where the survey ended.

President Kennedy celebrated the line's bicentennial in November 1963, by opening a newly completed section of Interstate 95 at the Maryland-Delaware border (now known as the John F. Kennedy Memorial Highway). It was his last public appearance. Eight days later, he was assassinated in Dallas.

Border disputes occur in chess games too, as in the diagram on the following page. In this game, Black has more pieces, but White has a better position. What is White's best move?

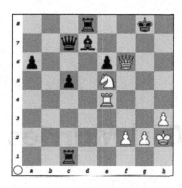

The solution to Puzzle #71 appears on Page 257.

So, do not wait for Maryland to annex Philadelphia. Do not wait for the next border dispute. Do not wait for the next celebration. Play chess now!

When a Girl Marries

October 20, 2017

Names are important to individuals. It is their identity--- personally and professionally. So when women marry, should they be required to take their husband's surname?

It has been the custom or law for many years, that when a woman marries, she changes her surname to that of her husband and their children bear the father's surname. In recent years, however, there is a trend toward equality of treatment of family names.

In some places women are not required or expected to take their husband's name and in some places, it is even forbidden. In Quebec, for example, a Provincial law requires people to keep their birth names for life. The law is based on a 1976 Charter of Rights, which extends gender equality to names. Greece adopted a similar law in 1983 during a wave of feminist legislation. Women, thus, use their maiden name after marriage. Iran has a similar system.

In France, a law on the books since 1789 requires that people not use a name besides the one on their birth certificate. Although women cannot legally change their surname after marriage, both husband and wife can accept the other's surname for social purposes. Similar laws apply in Italy, Netherlands, and Belgium. In Spain, Chile, Malaysia, and Korea, it is local custom for women to keep their maiden names. In Japan, married couples are required to take one of the spouses' family names; nearly all married women assume their husband's last name.

The European Union has been active in eliminating gender discrimination. A 1978 declaration by the Council of Europe requires member governments to take measures to adopt equality of rights in the transmission of family names. Such measures were taken by Germany, Sweden, Denmark, and Spain. In 2005, France adopted a measure that permits parents to give children the family name of the father, the mother, or a hyphenation of both. Previously, the law required children to take the surname of the father.

In 1979, the United Nations got into the naming act, establishing the Convention on the Elimination of All Forms of Discrimination Against Women (CEDAW). The Feminist Majority Foundation, a non-profit organization headquartered in Virginia, considers CEDAW to be the most comprehensive and detailed international agreement seeking the advancement of women.

With regard to surnames, the treaty states that wife and husband shall have equal rights to choose a family name. This is part of a long list of women's rights or gender equality rights specified in the treaty.

Although the United States was active in drafting the convention, it has not ratified the CEDAW, which has been ratified by 187 countries. President Carter signed the treaty in 1980, but Congress has not acted on it. Beside the U.S., six other countries have not ratified it--- the Pacific island nations of Tonga and Palau; Iran, Somalia, South Sudan and Sudan.

In the United States, more women in recent years have opted to keep their maiden names. According to the New York Times, 30% now keep their maiden names, compared to 14% in the 1980s and 18% in the 1990s.

Chess players are indifferent to names. They will play anyone, regardless of their name. They will even play anonymously against an opponent on the Internet. In the game pictured on the following page, it is White's move. White can capture the Black Knight on d5. Does White have a better move?

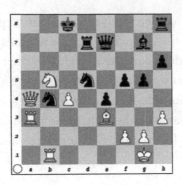

The solution to Puzzle #72 appears on Page 257.

So, do not wait for a marriage. Do not wait for an international convention. Do not wait for equality. Play chess now!

Chess Devotion Is More Than Skin-Deep

November 3, 2017

You can't buy kangaroo leather shoes in California, even though Australian kangaroos are no longer on the endangered species list. The state first prohibited the sale of kangaroo products in 1971, a year after banning products made from 23 other animals, including polar bears, zebras, whales, dolphins and elephants.

Soccer players prefer Kangaroo-skin shoes because of their flexibility, mobility, and comfort. The shoes, such as Adidas Predator, generally sell at higher prices than ordinary soccer shoes, about $200 a pair.

In 2003, a British-based animal-rights group with an office in Davis, California, called VIVA! (Vegetarians' International Voice for Animals), challenged Adidas, arguing that the California ban was valid because states have the power to enact stronger protections for wildlife than the federal government. The group argued that kangaroos are slaughtered cruelly and millions of kangaroos are killed every year in "what is widely regarded as the largest wildlife massacre on the planet."

A San Francisco Superior Court judge and the appeals court ruled in favor of Adidas in 2006, concluding that the law conflicted with a federal policy to resume imports in 1981 as a result of Australia's implementation of a program managing its kangaroo population. In 2007, the California Supreme Court, however, reversed the decision, thus upholding the law.

Despite the court decision, California's legislature enacted a moratorium in 2007, which was scheduled to expire at the end of 2015. Efforts by California businesses to remove the ban permanently failed, allowing the ban to be reinstated on 1 January 2016.

Nationally, the U.S. Fish and Wildlife Service (USFWS) originally had banned imports of kangaroo products in 1974, but allowed imports to resume in 1981 because the kangaroo population had increased to 35 million and Australia had imposed hunting quotas. In 1995, USFWS delisted kangaroos due to Australia's kangaroo population management program. The International Union for Conservation in Nature (IUCN), an international organization that monitors endangered species worldwide, has ruled that kangaroos are not threatened with extinction and classifies them in a category "of least concern."

Under Australia's commercial harvest program, there are no kangaroo farms; all kangaroos are killed at night in the wild by licensed marksmen, who follow a federal "Code of Practice for the Humane Shooting of Kangaroos," which requires a single bullet to the head.

The number killed each year for meat and skins is subject to quota limits, generally 10% of the population or roughly 2 million per year. The population of the harvest area averages about 25 million, but has been as high as 50 million in some years. Despite these harvests, the kangaroo population continues to grow. Some parts of Australia are overrun by kangaroos, which are regarded as pests in rural areas.

The kangaroo industry contributes to Australia's exports and overall economy with production valued at A$174 million (2014), generating 4,000 direct and indirect jobs, 2,000 of which are in the processing and transport sector in addition to allied jobs in government. Kangaroos also are recognized for their appeal to tourists.

Chess players do not need to wear kangaroo leather shoes to play their game. In the chess game on the following page, Black's King is in trouble on all sides, but it is Black's turn to move. What is Black's best move?

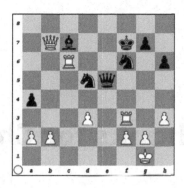

The solution to Puzzle #73 appears on Page 257.

So, do not wait for a hunting license. Do not wait for kangaroo shoes. Do not wait for an end to California's ban. Play chess now!

Giving Thanks for Chess

November 17, 2017

Thanksgiving is probably the least commercial of our holidays. Spending for costumes, candy, trees, and decoration is minimal, comparatively speaking. Spending (roughly $14 billion per year) is concentrated mostly on travel (to be with family) and on overeating.

Nearly 50 million Americans traveled 50 miles or more to be with family and friends last year, almost 90% by automobile. It is a time for people to gripe about traffic congestion.

It is also a time for tradition and turkeys. We try to observe Thanksgiving the way it was celebrated at Plymouth, Massachusetts in 1621 by the Pilgrims and the Wampanoag Indians, who feasted on fowl (probably wild turkeys) and fish. According to some historians, the first Thanksgiving was attended by 90 Native American Indians and 53 Pilgrims. The feast lasted for three days.

Raising turkeys is big business. This year we are expected to consume about 46 million turkeys. The supply is adequate, with about 300 million produced in the United States this year. Turkey is hardly an endangered species, except on Thanksgiving.

George Washington, as leader of the revolutionary forces in the American Revolutionary War, proclaimed a Thanksgiving in December 1777 as a victory celebration honoring the defeat of the British at Saratoga. Over the years, various Presidents (including Washington) issued Proclamations annually designating Thanksgiving as a November celebration. It has been celebrated as a federal holiday every year since 1863, when, during the Civil War, President Abraham Lincoln proclaimed a national day of Thanksgiving to be celebrated on the last Thursday in November.

In 1939, a year with five Thursdays in November, Franklin D. Roosevelt broke with tradition, proclaiming the fourth Thursday as Thanksgiving Day. Republicans criticized the change, calling it an affront to the memory of Lincoln. People began referring to November 30 as the "Republican Thanksgiving" and November 23 as the "Democratic Thanksgiving" or "Franksgiving." Finally, in December 1941, Congress enacted a law for the first time making Thanksgiving a legal federal holiday and setting the day as the fourth Thursday of November. Proclamations are no longer needed.

Thanksgiving is a time when we give thanks for what we have. Chess players, too, are thankful. By popular demand, here is our list of reasons to be thankful for chess. (This year's list has been expanded somewhat.)

1. It is safer than sky diving.
2. It requires only one other person to play (unless you play against the computer).
3. It is cheaper than playing the lottery.
4. It does not require costumes, uniforms, or safety equipment.
5. It keeps our minds off snack foods and everything else.
6. It is non-political.
7. There is no need to hit or chase a ball.
8. You don't need to know a foreign language.
9. It can be done without the help of government.
10. It is not fattening.
11. It won't get you into debt.
12. It does not require a password.
13. It is unaffected by fluctuating prices.
14. It can be played without batteries.
15. It gives us something to teach our grandchildren when they teach us how to use an i-phone or an i-pad.

Many chess tournaments are held during Thanksgiving. Chess players at Leisure World, however, do not need a holiday to play chess.

So, do not wait for the fifth Thursday of the month! Do not wait for a 3-day feast! Do not wait for traffic to ease! Play chess now!

Communicating in the Language of Chess

December 1, 2017

Esperanto Day is December 15, the birthday of L. L. Zamenhof, an eye-doctor, who invented the language. As a "constructed" easy-to-learn language, Esperanto was designed to serve as a second language for international communication.

Zamenhof introduced it in 1887 in a book published in Russian: "International Language: Introduction and Complete Textbook. Because Zamenhof used the pen name, "Doktoro Esperanto," people learning the language simply called it, Esperanto.

Historians had difficulty describing Zamenhof's ethnicity. Some called him a Polish Jew; some called him a Lithuanian Jew or a Russian Jew. He was born and lived in the Bialystok area of what is now Poland. Poland, then part of the Russian Empire, did not become an independent country until 1918--- one year after his death.

The "L.L." in his name also posed a problem because of language differences. Was it Ludwik Lazarz as in Polish; Lyudik Lazar "Leizer" (Russian); Ludwig Levi Lazarus (German); Ludwig Lazarus (English); or Ludviko Lazaro (Esperanto)?

Considering national pride in languages, Esperanto was not intended to replace national languages, but to augment them   as a second language or "neutral tongue." Zamenhof believed this would facilitate international communication, and thereby promote peace. According to estimates, about 150,000-300,000 people speak it proficiently today and up to two million people are familiar with it to some extent.

In the 1930's, both Hitler and Stalin banned the language. Hitler regarded it as part of "an international Jewish conspiracy." Portugal and Spain also banned it as "a threat to national purity." In some instances, it has been associated with communism as a "proletariat language" and with anarchy as a "nationless language." With the advent of the computer, as a practical matter English has become the world's second language.

Currently, the Universal Esperanto Association (UEA), headquartered in Rotterdam, organizes annual meetings, usually at the end of July, commemorating the anniversary of the language. The World Esperanto Congress meets in different countries each year, with participants averaging about 2,000 from 60 countries. UEA also publishes a magazine and books in Esperanto, and maintains a library. Through its office in New York City, it conducts relations with the United Nations, where UNESCO (UN Environmental, Scientific, and Cultural Organization) has granted "consultative status" to UEA.

As a classic international game, chess deserves to be included in an international language. You will be pleased to know, therefore, that Esperanto contains words for chess, all the chess pieces, and chess terms, such as checkmate, stalemate, and perpetual check. For example, *mortigas* is the word for checkmate (to immobilize) and the word for chess is *sako* (pronounced shahko).

In fact, chess enthusiasts in many countries embraced Esperanto as a means of reducing translation costs for international tournaments. Also, it was used for international chess publications and for notating chess moves in international correspondence between players.

You don't need to learn a foreign language to play chess at Leisure World. You don't need to shout or whisper. You don't need to speak at all.

In the diagram on this page, White's Queen is threatening Black's Pawn at b4, checking the King and capturing Black's Rook at a5. However, it is Black's turn to move. What is Black's best move?

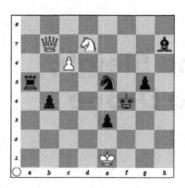

The solution to puzzle #74 appears on Page 257.

So, do not wait for next Esperanto Day. Do not wait for the Esperanto Congress to meet. Do not wait for another international language. Play chess now!

Forget the Sleigh;
Make It a Drone

December 15, 2017

'Twas the night before Christmas and it was freezing outside,
But Santa and his reindeer were enjoying the ride.

They cruised over fields and mountains with speed,
avoiding politicians' debates we don't really need.

Oblivious to the economy and political rifts,
Santa kept delivering the season's gifts.

No lumps of coal, but plenty of chess sets.
This was no time to think of taxes and debts.

So joy to you all. Keep the holiday spirit alive.
Don't worry about money. We'll all survive.

Commercially, to handle the Christmas mail, the U.S. Postal Service currently is making home deliveries seven or eight days a week. It expects to deliver 850 million packages during the holiday period this year. The major package delivery services also will deliver millions of packages: UPS estimates 700 million; FedEx, 360 million. The combined total approaches two billion packages, ten percent more than last year.

Santa Claus is planning to use new high-tech delivery methods so that he will have more time to play chess during the holiday season. The idea is to use specially equipped drones with arms to carry and drop off gift packages at designated locations identified by GPS coordinates.

Home deliveries are complicated. Not everyone lives in a detached single family home with a chimney. Santa will have to solve the problem of delivering to high-rise apartment buildings and condos in heavily populated areas. He will need exceptional creativity and, most of all, great imagination to make the system workable.

Further experiments are in progress, such as drone deliveries to secure stations where recipients can pick up packages, as well as store deliveries direct to the trunks of parked cars.

In February this year, CNN reported that the U.S. Patent and Trademark Office granted Amazon a patent for a method to guide packages released from drones safely to the ground using parachutes. This suggests that Amazon is considering keeping its drones high above customers' homes, which could be practical and safe. The patent document indicates that landing a drone takes more time and energy than releasing a package from the sky. The drone would monitor the package as it descends to assure that it lands safely.

A drone delivery system in the United States will require authorization by the Federal Aviation Administration (FAA). In designing regulations, the FAA must grapple with problems of air traffic control to avoid congestion and mid-air collisions and safety of civilians and their properties on the ground. Developing rules for air delivery by drones may not be that great a challenge for an agency that has developed rules for flying reindeer. Anything is possible.

Aside from drones, in the transportation field various companies are experimenting with driverless automobiles, automated trains, and unmanned cargo vessels, according to press reports. These developments, however, will take time and will provide no help to Santa this year. Poor Santa practically has no time to play chess this season.

Meanwhile, despite the holiday season, chess games continue at Leisure World, as illustrated by the diagram on this page. In this game, Black is in danger of checkmate by the White Rooks at a6 and b4, but it is Black's turn to move. What is Black's best move?

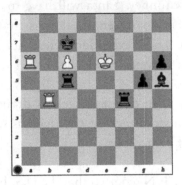

The solution to Puzzle #75 appears on Page 257.

So do not wait for delivery by drone. Do not wait for new FAA rules. Do not wait for Santa. Play chess now!

For Whom the Ball Drops

January 5, 2018

At 11:59 pm on New Year's Eve, the ball begins to drop at Times Square. Millions witness the descent on the streets or on television. It is a celebration of the passage of time, with expectations of a better year to come and resolutions to make that happen.

The ball has become a symbol of the holiday. It is now in public view year-round atop the building at One Times Square. The ball has been dropping each year since 1907 (except for the war years, 1942-43).

Times Square celebrations started in 1904, when Adolph Ochs (owner of the New York Times) purchased the building for the newspaper's new headquarters. At the time, the building was the tallest in Manhattan--- if measured from the bottom of its four massive sub-basements, built to support the heavy printing equipment.

Originally known as Longacre Square, Ochs successfully lobbied the City to change the name to Times Square. Around the same time, August Belmont, President of the Interborough Rapid Transit Company, suggested the name change, as the city opened its first subway line.

The first New Year's Eve celebration followed an all-day street festival with fireworks set off at the base of the tower at midnight. According to the New York Times, "the joyful sound of cheering, rattles, and noisemakers from the over 200,000 attendees could be heard...from as far away as Croton-on-Hudson, thirty miles north along the Hudson River."

Thus, Times Square replaced Lower Manhattan's Trinity Church as the focal point of New York's New Year celebration. Two years later, when the city banned the fireworks display, Ochs arranged to have an illuminated iron and wood ball lowered from the tower flagpole precisely at midnight to signal the beginning of 1908. The ball was 5 feet in diameter, weighed 700 pounds, and was illuminated by one hundred 25-watt light bulbs.

The nature of the ball has changed over the years. In 1920, a 400-pound ball made entirely of wrought iron replaced the original. In 1955, an aluminum ball weighing only 150 pounds replaced the iron ball. This aluminum ball remained unchanged until the 1980s. During the "I Love New York" marketing campaign (1981-88) the ball was made to look like an apple with red light bulbs and a green stem. The traditional white ball returned in 1989 without the green stem. In 1995, the ball was upgraded with aluminum skin, rhinestones, strobes, and computer controls.

To ring in the Year 2000, the ball was completely redesigned by Waterford Crystal and Philips Lighting. The crystal ball combined the latest in lighting technology with the most traditional of materials to celebrate the new millennium.

In 2007, for the 100th anniversary of the Ball Drop tradition, a new LED crystal ball was designed, replacing the incandescent and halogen bulbs of the past century. The ball, now 12 feet in diameter and weighing nearly 12,000 pounds, is adorned with 2,688 Waterford Crystal triangles, illuminated by 32,256 Philips Luxeon LEDs (light emitting diodes), greatly increasing its brightness and color capabilities. It is now a permanent feature of the building at One Times Square.

Predictably, chess players at Leisure World resolve to play better next year. They do not need a holiday or a big celebration to play. In the game pictured on the following page, Black's Queen has just captured a Pawn at c5. What is White's best move?

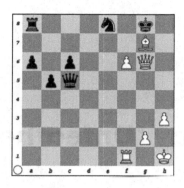

The Solution to Puzzle# 76 appears on Page 257.

So, do not wait for a spectacular celebration. Do not wait for a ball to drop. Do not wait until next year. Play chess now!

Chess Play 'Unfeathered' by Birds

January 18, 2018

The Chinese New Year, which begins on February 16, and is known as the Year of the Dog, may be more widely recognized, but 2018 has already been designated by National Geographic as "The Year of the Bird."

In conjunction with other birdlife organizations, the magazine will be celebrating the centennial of the Migratory Bird Treaty Act of 1918.

The Migratory Bird Treaty sounds like a government visa program with a quota limitation on immigration of birds. However, it is not. Birds are free to fly wherever they want.

The treaty, negotiated with Britain (representing Canada), is an agreement not to kill birds, or more specifically, to conserve them by making it illegal to kill them. The Act also bans hunting, capturing, and selling about 800 species listed as migratory birds.

Exceptions are made in certain cases. For example, U.S. Fish and Wildlife Service (FWS) issues permits that allow Native Americans to use birds for religious ceremonies. FWS also issues permits for taxidermy, falconry, propagation, scientific and educational use, as well as depredation permits to prevent bird attacks or to kill geese near an airport, where they pose a danger to aircraft.

The bird population on the planet is estimated to be 200 to 400 billion, many times larger than the human population (roughly 8 billion), but the number of birds has been declining for many years.

It is estimated that 14% of all species will become extinct by 2100, according to an ornithologist from the Center for Biodiversity and Conservation of the American Museum of Natural History.

As stated in the January issue, National Geographic magazine will feature stories about birds all year long, examining "how our changing environment is leading to dramatic losses among bird species around the globe…our last, best connection to a natural world that is otherwise receding."

Birds bring natural beauty to the world. Many are scavengers, serving as the world's sanitation corps, devouring dead animals, insects, rodents, and crop pests. Some pollinate plants and spread seeds of many plants, including crops important to humans. Seabirds and bats produce guano used for fertilizer.

Millions of seabirds live in the Chincha Islands off the coast of Peru, producing excrement (guano) rich in nitrates and phosphates. Guano covered the islands with a coating 200 feet deep. This became a valuable source of fertilizer for American farmers in the 1840's. Ships carried thousands of tons of guano to the United States. If we could train seabirds to fly over the farms that need fertilizer, lots of money could be saved on transportation costs.

Try explaining these benefits to the people who are afraid of birds and hate birds. Three million Americans suffer from ornithophobia (an intense, irrational fear of birds) and many others feel uncomfortable in the presence of birds. People hate birds for a variety of reason. They splatter automobile windshields, fly into jet engines causing airplane crashes, chew manicured golf greens, make a mess of garbage bags, and spread diseases, such as the black plague and avian flu.

Birds and aircraft do not disturb chess games at Leisure World. Chess players feel comfortable because birds do not attack chess players, especially when they play indoors.

In the game pictured on this page, Black is winning, but it is White's turn to move. What is White's best move?

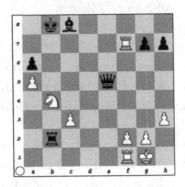

The solution to Puzzle #77 appears on page 257.

So, do not wait for Chinese New Year. Do not wait for more bird migration. Do not wait for a boatload of guano. Play chess now!

The War of 1812

February 2, 2018

The War of 1812 is over, but its bicentennial celebration lives on. The war is generally regarded as America's most indecisive and unnecessary war. It remains alive in the hearts and minds of historians because the burning of the White House and composition of the Star Spangled Banner are unforgettable events.

Yet many of us have forgotten the toll of this war on James Madison, an ardent chess player. On occasion, he played chess with Thomas Jefferson and James Monroe, both of whom lived a carriage ride away from his home in Montpelier, Virginia.

James Madison served as the fourth President of the United States from 1809 to 1817. He was small in physical stature, only 5-foot-four and 100 pounds. He was frail and had a high, thin voice. Dolley Payne Todd, 3 inches taller and 17 years younger, married him anyway. He had to bear the burden of the War of 1812 and other problems of office, a formidable responsibility for such a short, delicate person.

In January 1814, President Madison had agreed to peace talks with the British in Ghent, Belgium, a neutral country. Nevertheless, the war continued.

In the most embarrassing point of the war (August 1814), 4,000 British troops landed at Benedict, Maryland, on the Patuxent River, marched to Bladensburg, where they defeated a larger force of American militiamen,

237

and then marched to Washington, where they burned the Capitol, the President's Mansion (the White House) and other buildings. James and Dolley fled to a safer location. In September, they moved to the Octagon House, a few streets away (18th & New York Avenue).

That month, the British attacked Baltimore with land and sea forces. Francis Scott Key, a lawyer and amateur poet (not a songwriter), was on board a British troop ship during the bombardment of Fort McHenry. He was there to free an American citizen who was detained by the British. They were released after the battle.

Key was inspired to write a poem about the U.S. flag on the back of a letter he had in his pocket. The flag, which survived the battle, had 15 stars and 15 stripes (8 red, 7 white) and was quite large, measuring 30 by 42 feet. It cost $405.90.

Key's poem was printed in newspapers and eventually set to music. People began referring to the song as "The Star-Spangled Banner." In 1889, the U.S. Navy adopted it for official use and in 1916 President Woodrow Wilson announced that it should be played at all official events. On March 3, 1931, it was adopted as the national anthem by congressional resolution, signed by President Herbert Hoover.

Francis Scott Key never got to meet President Madison. The frail President died in 1836 at age 85. Key died in 1843 at 64 and Dolley died in 1849 at 81.

Because historians tell us very little about it, we are only left to wonder how much Madison's official duties interfered with his chess playing. When would he have time to play a relaxing game and relieve his mind of all those troubles of the Presidency?

In the game on the following page, Black's Rook is threatening White's Queen. What is White's best move? (Note: there are two solutions.)

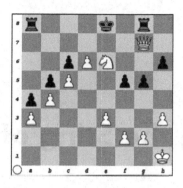

The solution to Puzzle #78 appears on Page 257.

So, do not wait for a new Presidential Mansion. Do not wait for another war. Do not wait for a brass band to play the national anthem. Play chess now!

Avoiding the Sting of Defeat

February 16, 2018

Bees know how to fly--- even though they defy the laws of gravity and aeronautics. By studying bee flight in slow motion, scientists think they know how it is done. Evidently, bees are able to lift their own weight off the ground by flapping their little wings many, many times and quickly (about 11,400 times per minute).

Their flight does not depend on what they eat. During the summer bees eat nectar of flowers and fertilize them at the same time. They make honey and store it for the winter when few flowers are available for food. Honey made by honeybees can be stored indefinitely without going bad. It is okay for humans to take some of the honey as long as it is plentiful. Presumably, beekeepers know how much to take without harming the bees.

Bumblebees are different than honeybees and they do not make the same kind of honey--- the honey used by humans. Bumblebee honey is stored as nectar for only a short time because their colonies do not last as long as honeybee colonies. Bumblebees live in nests with 50-400 bees; honeybees live in hives with up to 50,000-60,000 bees. Honeybees have to feed a colony of workers plus the queen throughout the winter; bumblebees feed only the queen, who survives while the rest of the colony dies in the winter.

In looks, honeybees are distinguished from bumblebees by their many stripes with several gray ones at the tip of the abdomen. Bumblebees are more broad and furry with blocks of color rather than a series of stripes. Bees themselves know the difference immediately.

Female honeybees and bumblebees both sting, but honeybee stingers are barbed and bumblebee stingers are not. Thus, when honeybees sting, they lose their stingers and die, whereas bumblebees retain their stingers and may sting several times. Male bees do not have stingers, another example of gender inequality in nature.

Carpenter bees are often mistaken for bumblebees. They are a separate species approximately the same size as the bumblebee, but with less hair on their abdomen and no yellow markings. They are considered a threat to human dwellings because they drill holes into wood decks and overhangs to leave their eggs. These holes cause weaknesses in the structure. Female carpenter bees are not aggressive, but they will sting if they feel their nests are threatened.

Giant honeybees are found in Nepal in Himalayan mountain overhangs hundreds of feet above the ground. Their bodies are nearly an inch long, compared to most other bees, which are roughly two-thirds of an inch. Honey hunters climb rope ladders to saw off crescent-shaped hives with thousands of giant bees. The bees produce a sticky, reddish fluid, known as mad honey, which is said to have hallucinogenic properties. Mad honey sells for $60-$80 a pound on Asia's black markets, roughly six times the price of regular Nepali honey, according to National Geographic. For centuries this honey has been used as a cough syrup, as an antiseptic, and sometimes as a sexual stimulant.

Chess players at Leisure World do not want to be stung by their opponent's moves on the chessboard. In the game pictured on the following page, White has just stung Black by capturing the Pawn at b7, threatening to capture the Rook at a8 and become a Queen. What is Black's best move?

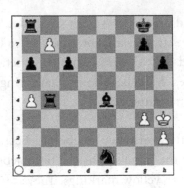

The solution to Puzzle # 79 appears on Page 257.

So, do not wait for scientific proof that bees can fly. Do not wait for hallucinogenic honey. Do not wait for extinction of carpenter bees. Play chess now!

Intangible Culture, Intangible Chess

March 2, 2018

We live in a disposable world. We don't take care of old things or fix them. We throw them away and get new ones to replace them. We are accustomed to living this way.

Bucking the trend is difficult, but there is an international organization dedicated to protecting beloved old cultural and natural sites. It is UNESCO, the United Nations Education, Scientific, and Cultural Organization. Its World Heritage Committee manages the program and maintains lists of these sites based on a 1972 international convention, ratified by 193 countries. The objective is to conserve historic sites for posterity by protecting them from commercialization, decay, and destruction.

Since 1975, when the convention came into force, 1,073 sites in 167 countries have been registered (as of July 2017). Italy has the greatest number of registered sites (53), but China is a close second with 52. The United States is tenth with 23.

Italy's sites include historic centers of Florence, Naples and Rome (including the Holy See), Venice and its Lagoon, and Pisa. China's include the Great Wall and the Ming Tombs. The United States' includes the Grand Canyon, the Statue of Liberty, and, most recently, the Alamo. Listing a site on the Register confers official status to the site as a protected zone.

In addition to buildings, monuments and other physical sites, in 2001, UNESCO began maintaining a list of *intangible* cultural heritage to raise awareness of customs and traditions and to encourage local communities to protect them. These intangibles include national cuisines (French, Mexican and Japanese); dances: flamenco (Spain), tango (Argentina, Uruguay), rumba (Cuba); bullfighting (Spain); beer (Belgium) and Yoga (India).

Can chess be far behind? As a matter of fact, in 2014, the Presidents of the European Chess Union and the French Chess Federation met with UNESCO's Director-General to discuss recognition of chess as an intangible world heritage. Evidently no action has been taken since then.

However, a German chess village (Ströbeck) is recognized by the German Commission for UNESCO, which maintains its own Inventory of Intangible Cultural Heritage. Chess has been at the heart of Ströbeck life since the year 1011. The village developed its own rules, including special moves, additional pieces, cryptic commands, and a board with 96 squares. Beginning in 1823, chess education has been mandatory in primary schools. Prospective grooms are required to play chess against the mayor in order to win their bride. One groom who lost to the mayor had to pay €70 to the chess club to marry his bride. UNESCO is likely to add this to its registry some day.

Cultures can also be removed from the list, as in the case of Viennese balls, an Austrian tradition and a highlight of the social calendar, where eligible bachelors waltz with glamorous debutants during the first months of the year. An Austrian culture committee, in 2012, recommended removal due to public pressure from critics who claim that the Ball des Wiener Korporationsringes, known as the WKR-Ball attracts neo-Nazis from across Europe.

Chess players at Leisure World are keeping the game alive without UNESCO protection. So do not wait for an international convention. Do not wait to play a game with the mayor. Do not wait for UNESCO recognition. Play chess now!

How to Dress for Chess

March 16, 2018

Fashion has not yet corrupted the chess world. Fashion designers are missing out on a potentially large untapped market. Just think of all the business that could be generated by convincing chess players that they need three wardrobe changes a day to be stylish.

Hollywood has projected a false image for chess. In "From Russia with Love," for example, two men (who are actually spies) are dressed elegantly in custom-tailored black tuxedos with black ties to compete in a chess match. They sit at a table on a raised circular platform in the center of a ballroom in a swanky hotel, underneath a magnificent chandelier. The tile floor itself is configured as a giant chessboard.

For the audience, packed around the sides of the room, a wall-length board displays the position of the pieces. Guests in the audience are wearing fine, formal attire: ladies in gowns, men in tuxedos. They sip from cocktail glasses, anxiously awaiting the next move. After each move, an attendant, dressed immaculately in black tie and tails, moves the pieces on the magnetic wall board to reflect the current status of the game.

In real life, players in chess tournaments generally prefer casual clothing to suits and ties or tuxedos. Players feel more relaxed in casual clothes and better able to think clearly. On the other hand, players in casual clothes may feel intimidated by opponents wearing elegant outfits. So formal wear might give a psychological edge to some chess players.

The European Chess Union specifies dress rules for chess players during tournaments. Generally, the rules allow almost anything appropriate to be worn as long as it does not show "excessive wear, or holes," and is "free of body odor." Beachwear is not appropriate, but national costumes can be worn "as long as they are not indecent or offensive to others."

Men are to wear "trousers or jeans, a long-sleeve or short-sleeve dress shirt, alternatively T-shirt or polo, loafers or dressy slip-ons, socks, shoes or sneakers…and, if appropriate, a sport coat or blazer. Glasses and neckties can be worn, but not caps or hats, except for religious purposes."

Women are to wear "blouses, turtleneck, T-shirts or polos, trousers, jeans or slacks, skirts, dresses, and appropriate footwear (boots, flats, mid-heel or high-heel shoes, sneakers) or any other appropriate clothing. "A jacket vest or sweater, as well as jewelry (earrings, necklace, etc.) coordinated to the outfit may be worn."

Nevertheless, there is no official dress code for non-tournament chess, particularly in Clubhouse II on a weekday afternoon.

From their fierce battles on the chessboard, you might expect Leisure World players to wear protective clothing, perhaps a suit of armor and a metallic shield--- at least helmets, shoulder pads and shin guards. However, this is not the case. It is safe to play as all the action takes place on the chessboard and in the minds of the combatants.

Despite the glamour of the game, Leisure World chess players are usually seen wearing casual attire --- jeans, slacks and short-sleeved shirts, sweaters, even shorts, polo shirts, and occasionally, Redskin sweatshirts. No uniforms are required.

If by chance, you happen to see women in gowns and men in tuxedos in the clubhouse, you will know that either *they* are in the wrong place or *you* are in the wrong place.

So, do not wait for Hollywood. Do not wait for next year's fashions. Do not wait for uniforms. Play chess now!

Solutions to Puzzles

#1
White's best move is Pawn to f7. This puts Black's King in check, opens the diagonal for White's Queen and forces Black's King to capture the Pawn at f7. Then White moves the Queen to g7. Checkmate!

#2
Black moves the Queen to f4. Checkmate!

#3
Black moves the Rook to f2. Checkmate!

#4
Black moves the Rook to e1. Checkmate!

#5
Black does not have a good move. Black's King is trapped. No matter what he moves, he loses the game by checkmate on the next move. White moves the Rook to c6 for the checkmate!

#6
Black moves the Rook at d8 to d1, checking the King. White can only defend by moving the Queen to e1. Black then captures the Queen. Checkmate!

#7
White moves the Rook from g7 to g3 or g4 or simply move the Queen to h7. Checkmate!

#8

White can win the game simply by moving the Knight from d2 to f3. Checkmate!

#9

White wins by moving the Rook to a1, checkmate!

#10

White can win the game by moving the Queen to e7. Black's Queen cannot capture the White Queen because it is pinned by the Rook. Knight to f6 also wins for White. Checkmate!

#11

White can win the game by moving the Knight from e3 to d5, checking the King. The King's only move is to d8. White then moves the Bishop at f4 to either c7 or g5. Checkmate!

#12

In the actual game, Black chose to capture White's Queen at c3 with the Knight from e4. He had a better move, however. He could have moved the Knight to f2. Checkmate!

#13

Black can settle for a draw by keeping the White King in perpetual check, moving the Queen to g4 (check) and to c4 (check) if White moves the King to f1 and so on. Black can also set up a possible trade of Queens at e4, but this is a riskier approach.

#14

White has a choice of many good moves, but the best is Bishop to d3. Checkmate!

#15

White's Knight captures the Pawn at f6, forcing Black's Bishop to g8 to protect against checkmate by the Queen at h7. White follows by moving the Knight to h5 (threatening mate by the Queen at g7). Black captures the Knight with the Pawn. White's Queen then moves to f6. Checkmate!

#16

Black can win the game by moving the Rook to d7, checkmate! (The White King cannot capture the Rook because it is protected by the Bishop at a4).

#17

White can win the game by moving the Knight from g7 to e6, double check. Black must move the King to e8. White follows with Queen to f8, check. Black captures White's Queen by the Knight from g6. The White Knight at e6 then moves back to g7, checkmate! The Black King is trapped at e8 because f8, which would have been a safe square, is now occupied by the Black Knight. Checkmate!

#18

White can win the game by moving the Rook to h8, checking the King. Black's King captures the Rook. White moves the Queen to h6 and checks the King. Black cannot capture the Queen because the Pawn at g7 is pinned by White's Bishop at a1. Thus, Black must move the King to g8, whereupon White's Queen captures the Pawn at g7 and wins the game. Checkmate!

#19

White can win the game by moving the Rook to d8, checking the King. Black can block by moving the Knight to e8, but it is then captured by the Rook. Checkmate!

#20

White can save the Rook, but must keep it in the first row to prevent checkmate by Black's Queen at g1. But it is better for White to move the Knight from f5 to e7. Checkmate!

#21

White moves the Queen to g8, checking the King. Black can only interpose the Queen at f8. White then captures the Queen. Checkmate!

#22

Black can move the Queen to b1. After that, no matter what White does, Black then can win the game by moving the Queen to g1 or h1. Checkmate!

#23

The White Queen moves to b8. Checkmate!

#24

Black's best move is to capture White's Rook at f1 with the Queen, checking White's King, which then captures the Black Queen. On the next move, however, Black wins the game by moving the Rook from d8 to d1. Checkmate! (White can interpose the Knight, which would be captured on the next move by Black's Rook. Checkmate!)

#25

Black's Queen captures the Pawn at h2, checking the King, which moves to f1. Black's Queen then moves to h1. Checkmate!

#26

The game played out with White moving the Pawn at f2 to f4, threatening Black's Knight. Black responded by capturing White's Rook at d1. White then captured Black's Knight at e5 with the Bishop, threatening Black's Queen. Black moved the Queen to b6. White followed by moving the Queen to h8, checkmate!

#27

Black can beat White to the punch by capturing the Pawn at b2 with the Queen from e2. Checkmate!

#28

White first moves the Queen to h4, checking Black's King. Black captures White's Queen with the Queen from e7. White then captures Black's Queen with the Rook from f4. Checkmate!

#29

White can avoid checkmate by moving the King to d1. Thus, if Black moves either Rook to a1 or h1, White can interpose either of the Rooks at c3 or e5.

#30

White can win this game by sacrificing the Rook, moving it from b1 to b8. If Black captures the Rook with the Queen, it will no longer protect the e7 square. White's Queen can then move there without being captured. Checkmate! If Black chooses not to capture the Rook, White can still move the Queen to e7 because Black's Queen is pinned by White's Rook. Black, therefore, cannot capture White's Queen at e7. Checkmate!

#31

White moves the Knight from e3 to d5, checking the Black King, which can only move to d8. White then moves the Bishop to g5. Checkmate!

#32

White Knight (at g5) captures Black Pawn at f7. Checkmate!

#33

Black's best move is Rook at a8 to a1, check. White can block the Rook by bringing the Knight from e3 to d1, but Black's Rook can capture it on the next move. Checkmate!

#34

White can win the game by moving the Knight at f7 to h6, capturing Black's Pawn and uncovering a check from White's Rook at f1. Checkmate! White wins!

#35

White moves the Rook at c3 to c7, checking the King, and forcing Black to move it to the eighth rank. Thus, the King is no longer protecting the Black Knight at f6. White's Bishop is now able to capture the Knight and is in position to do more damage to Black's remaining Pawns. In this game, Black resigned after capture of the Knight.

#36

White can win the game by moving the Knight to b6. Checkmate!

#37

White actually won this game on the next move. The Knight at d7 is moved to f6, forking the King at g8 and the Queen at d5. It was not checkmate, but Black would lose the Queen and, therefore, resigned!

#38

It is best for White to move the Queen to f5, checking Black's King. Black has no choice and must move the King to h6, whereupon White counters by moving the Pawn to g5, checkmate! Thus, even though the situation looked bleak, White was able to force checkmate in two moves!

#39

Yes. Black had a much better move. Black could have moved the Queen to h1. Checkmate! Black could have won the game on that move.

#40

Black's best move is Queen to d2, Checkmate! Black wins the game!

#41

Black's best move is King to g5. This sets up a checkmate on the next move: Bishop to g2. Checkmate! (If Black's Bishop captures the Pawn at d7, the Bishop would be captured by the White Rook at d3.)

#42

White moves the Bishop to d7, checking the King. This forces Black to capture the Bishop with the King or Rook, whereupon White captures Black's Queen (at c5) and easily wins the game.

#43

White can win the game by moving the Rook to h8. Checkmate! (Interposing the Black Queen and Bishop do not help.)

#44

Black has little chance of winning this game. If Black captures White's Knight, White's Queen captures the Pawn at b7. Checkmate! If Black moves the King, White's Knight captures the Queen. What a predicament!

#45

White can move the Knight to e7, check. Black has to move the King to h8. White then captures the Black Queen. Checkmate!

#46

White has a devastating move: Pawn to f6! This threatens checkmate by the Queen at g7. Black's Pawn at g7 cannot capture White's Pawn because it would expose the Black King to check by the Queen. Black can prevent checkmate by moving the Pawn to g6, but that allows the White Pawn to capture the Rook at e7 and even the Queen at d8 and the Rook at f8. Moreover, while the White Pawn is at f6, the Queen can move to h6 and checkmate the King by moving to g7. Black is virtually helpless.

#47

White has an advantage and should win this game after Black encounters zugswang. When White moves the Pawn to f3, Black has only one "safe" move: Pawn to f6. White can then play Pawn to h3, creating a zugzwang. Black must move the King protecting the Pawn at b5, which is captured by White's King. Eventually, White can promote the Pawn at b4 to a Queen and win the game.

#48

If White's King moves to e3, Black checkmates on the next move, Qh6. If White captures the Bishop with the Rook, Black captures the Rook with a Pawn, checking the King. Actually, White has no good move. He can only hope for Black to blunder. If the White King moves to f1, Black moves to check the King at h1. White can then interpose the Rook from g3 to g1. Black then sacrifices the Queen, by capturing the Rook at g1. White's King captures the Queen at g1, but Black then moves the Rook from h8 to h1. Checkmate!

#49

Black should move the Knight to f3. Checkmate!

#50

Black has two good moves: Rook to h2 or Bishop to e8. Both result in checkmate!

#51

White moved the Rook from h3 to g3 to avert a checkmate at g1. Thus, the checkmate took place by moving the Black Queen to h1. Black's Knight at d4 is blocking the King's exit at f2 and c2 (if the King moves to d1). The King, therefore, is trapped. There is no way to stop the checkmate. Black wins with the Queen moving to g1 (if the White Rook remains stationary) or to h1 (if the Rook moves to g3). Checkmate!

#52

White's best move is Rook to b8. Black's Rook cannot move away from g8 to capture the White Rook because White's Queen can then capture the Pawn at g7, checkmate! If Black moves the Pawn from a3 to a2 to promote it to a Queen, it would be too late because then White's Queen can capture the Pawn at g7, checkmate! Black's Rook cannot capture the Queen because it is pinned and would expose the King to check by the White Rook. Black can prolong the game by moving the King to h7, but will lose the Rook and be checkmated by the Queen on the next move. Checkmate!

#53

Yes. Black moves the Knight to f3, forcing the King to moves to h5. Black's Rook then moves to g5. Checkmate!

#54

White can move the Bishop from c6 to e8, checking the King. Black can interpose the Queen, which then can be captured by White's Queen or Bishop, resulting in checkmate!

#55

White moves the Queen to h6, check. Black must move the King to g8. White then moves the Bishop from c6 to d5, checkmate!

#56

White moves the Rook from h7 to f7, check. Black can only move the King to e8. White moves the Rook from c7 to e7. Checkmate!

#57

White can move the Rook to g6, checking the King. Black can interpose the Queen at g7, which would then be captured by White's Queen, checkmate

#58

White moves the Rook to d7, threatening the Black Queen and checkmate. Black moves the Queen to e4. White then moves its Queen to f7, checking the King. Black moves the King to h8. White's Queen then captures the Bishop at f8, checkmate!

#59

White can win in one move. Queen moves to h7, checkmate! (Note that Black's Knight cannot capture the Queen because it is pinned by White's Bishop at b2.)

#60

White moves the Pawn to e8, promoting it to a Queen. Black captures the new Queen with the Rook from b8. White then captures the Rook with the old Queen from g6. Checkmate!

#61

Black's best move is Rook to h1. Checkmate!

#62

Black should move the Rook from c4 to h4. Checkmate!

#63

White moves the Bishop from g6 to h5. Checkmate!

#64

Black moves the Knight to e5. Checkmate!

#65

(1) White's Queen captures the Black Queen at d8, checking the King. Black's Knight captures the Queen. White follows with Rook to f8. Checkmate! (2) White moves the Rook to f8, checking the King. Black's only move is to capture the Rook with the Queen, whereupon White captures the Black Queen at f8. Checkmate!

#66

Black moves the Knight to g4, checking the White King. The King can move only to g1 or h1, whereupon Black moves the Rook to d1. Checkmate!

#67

White captures Black's Pawn at h7, double-checking the King. The Black King captures the White Pawn at h7, whereupon White's Queen moves to g7. Checkmate!

#68

White's Rook at c1 captures the Black Pawn at c6, checking the King. Black's Bishop captures the Rook. White's Queen then captures the Bishop. Black's King can move to b8 or d8. Either way, White moves the Rook to a8. Checkmate!

#69

Black moves the Rook from g2 to d2. Checkmate!

#70

Black's best move is King to f5, limiting the spaces where White's King can move. In this game, White followed by capturing Black's Pawn at b6. Black then moved the Rook from d1 to d3. Checkmate! (Note that White could have avoided checkmate, at least temporarily, by moving the Rook from a6 to a3).

#71

White moves the Queen to f7, checking the King. Black's King moves to h8, whereupon White moves the Rook to h4. Checkmate!

#72

Yes. Queen to a8. Checkmate!

#73

Black's Queen moves to e1. Checkmate!

#74

Black moves the Rook to a1, checking the King and forcing White to move the King to e2. Black then moves the Bishop to d3. Checkmate!

#75

Black moves the Bishop to g4, checking the King. White's only move is to e7. Black follows by moving the Rook from c5 to e5. Checkmate!

#76

White moves the Pawn to f7. Checkmate!

#77

White moves the Knight to c6, forcing the Black King to move to a8. White then moves the Rook from f7 to a7. Checkmate!

#78

White moves Pawn to d7, or Queen to e7. Checkmate!

#79

Black moves the Bishop to g2. Checkmate!

About the Author

Bernard Ascher retired from the federal government after 42 years of service. As an international economist, he contributed to trade policy formulation and participated in international trade negotiations. A graduate of Brooklyn College (B.A./Economics) and City University of New York (M.B.A/International Trade), he taught international business courses as an Adjunct Professor at George Mason University and at University of Maryland University College. In addition to teaching, his post-retirement activities include consulting for the World Bank and other clients; writing publications as a fellow for the American Antitrust Institute ("Global Beer: The Road to Monopoly" and "The Audit Industry: World's Weakest Oligopoly"); and serving on the board of trustees of a non-profit organization. He and his late wife, Elinor, moved to Leisure World in 2006. His three children (Scott, Ruth and Mark) and five grandchildren (David, Jason, Jacob, Shayna, and Tyler) live in Montgomery County, Maryland.

Printed in the United States
By Bookmasters